KOREA: SECURITY PIVOT IN NORTHEAST ASIA

KOREA: SECURITY PIVOT IN NORTHEAST ASIA

by

Project Editor and Principal Author: Robert Dujarric
Research Fellow, Hudson Institute

Co-author: Kim Changsu, Ph.D.
Director, Office of Regional Military Affairs
Korea Institute for Defense Analyses

Co-author: Elizabeth A. Stanley
Harvard University

Project Director: Lt. Gen. William E. Odom, USA (ret.)
Director, National Security Studies, Hudson Institute

Hudson Institute
Indianapolis, Indiana

ISBN 1-55813-064-0
Copyright © 1998 Hudson Institute, Inc.

The cover depicts *Jakho-do* (magpie and tiger). Traditionally, the magpie symbolized good news. The Chinese symbol for leopard, which resembles the tiger, is pronounced (pyo) and another Chinese symbol, which means 'reporting good news' (po). These are almost homophonic to a Korean's ear. Therefore, the magpie and the tiger transfigured from a leopard make an allegorical picture. Art courtesy of MINHWA-Korean Folk Art Prints © 1994 Editions API, Seoul, Korea.

The views in this book are solely the views of the authors. No opinions, statements of fact, or conclusions contained in this document can be properly attributed to Hudson Institute, its staff, its members, its contracting agencies, or the other institutions with which the authors are affiliated.

Printed in the United States of America

This book may be ordered from:
Hudson Institute
Herman Kahn Center
5395 Emerson Way
Indianapolis, Indiana 46226 U.S.A.
phone: (317) 545-1000
fax: (317) 545-9639
1-800-HUDSON-Ø
www.hudson.org

TABLE OF CONTENTS

Acknowledgments

First and foremost, we would like to thank The Korea Foundation for its generous support of this project. The research for this book, as well as the Hudson Institute Conference in November 1996 on Capitol Hill on "Korea: Security Pivot in Northeast Asia," was made possible by a grant from The Korea Foundation.

Representative Lee Dong-bok and Dr. Thomas Park kindly introduced Hudson Institute to The Korea Foundation and Hudson Institute owes them a debt of gratitude for their assistance.

We held the conference in Washington in November 1996 on the topic of Northeast Asian security which we organized thanks to the organizational skills of Vice President of External Affairs, Craig Whitney, and Director of Special Events, Teresa Rhodes. Dr. Kongdan Oh, Dr. Kil Jeong-Woo, and Hudson Institute Senior Fellow Dr. Thomas J. Duesterberg kindly agreed to participate and to make presentations which contributed much to our understanding of Northeast Asia.

Our research was made much easier thanks to the efforts and assistance of the Hudson Institute Library and its superb staff. Deborah Jones, Gwen Rosen, and Gayle Crouse deserve much credit for making this book possible. Erica Mayer, an intern at Hudson Institute, helped put together the bibliography with much diligence and efficiency.

In Washington D.C., Denise Braye and Eva Grace provided us with secretarial assistance and we are very thankful for their help.

The Taipei Economic and Cultural Representative Office (TECRO) of the Republic of China in Washington, and its Secretariat Division, made possible a very informative visit by Hudson Institute researchers to Taiwan.

The U.S. Army War College Outreach Program made possible a very informative visit to the National Training Center at Fort Irwin, California, which was a fascinating demonstration of modern military exercises.

Dr. Gary Geipel, former Director of Research at Hudson Institute, also assisted us in drafting the initial project and helped us throughout the project. Robert Champ edited the book with great talent and speed, and Sam Karnick, Hudson Institute Director of Publications, guided the entire project from its inception to completion.

Obviously, we are solely responsible for any remaining errors and omissions. The views expressed in this book do not necessarily reflect the opinion of The Korea Foundation or of any the institutions with which the authors are affiliated.

REMARKS

Korean, Japanese, and Chinese personal names are written with the family name before the given name. In this book we have followed East Asian practice, with the exception of authors whose names are written in the western order (i.e. family name last) in the titles of their publications in western languages.

Chinese names are written according to the Pinyin system now in use in the People's Republic of China except when there is a different transcription in generally accepted English usage. Chinese names from areas outside of the PRC are transcribed according to local usage, generally the Wade-Gilles method which prevailed in the English-speaking world before the advent of Pinyin.

Whenever possible, economic and demographic data is from "The World in Figures" section of *The World in 1997* published by The Economist Newspaper in November 1996. The data are forecast from the Economist Intelligence Unit for 1997. They are thus only based on estimates but have the advantage of being current, as opposed to official statistics which often lag by a few years.

Unless otherwise indicated, "$" refers to U.S. dollars.

The contents of some chapters are adapted from *Hudson Briefing Papers* published earlier as noted in the appropriate endnotes.

ABBREVIATIONS AND ACRONYMS

APEC:	Asia-Pacific Economic Cooperation
ARF:	ASEAN Regional Forum (ASEAN countries and other countries)
ASEAN:	Association of Southeast Asian Nations
CBM:	Confidence Building Measures
CCP:	Chinese Communist Party (of the PRC)
DMZ:	Demilitarized Zone (between South and North Korea)
DPRK:	Democratic People's Republic of Korea (North Korea)
EU:	European Union
G-7:	The group of seven leading market economies (USA, Japan, Germany, France, Italy, UK, and Canada).
GDP:	Gross Domestic Product
KEDO:	Korean Peninsula Energy Development Organization
KMT:	Kuomintang (ruling Nationalist Party of the ROC)
LDP:	Liberal Democratic Party (of Japan)
LWR:	Light Water (nuclear) Reactor
MIA:	(Servicemen) Missing In Action
NATO:	North Atlantic Treaty Organization
OECD:	Organization for Economic Cooperation and Development (USA, Canada, Mexico, Western and some Central European nations, Japan, South Korea, Australia, New Zealand)
PLA:	People's Liberation Army (of the PRC)
POW:	Prisoner of War
PRC:	People's Republic of China (mainland China)
ROC:	Republic of China (on Taiwan)
ROK:	Republic of Korea (South Korea)
SDF:	Self Defense Forces (Japanese armed services)
U.S.:	United States of America
USFJ:	United States (armed) Forces in Japan
USFK:	United States (armed) Forces in (South) Korea
USSR:	Union of Soviet Socialist Republics (Soviet Union)

CHAPTER ONE
INTRODUCTION

Korea is the security pivot of Northeast Asia because there is a high likelihood of major change on the Korean peninsula, where the interests of the United States, Japan, China, and Russia intersect and have fueled international rivalries for over a century. It is the working hypothesis of this study that, over the next ten years, the status quo in Korea will be profoundly altered, either by a radical transformation in inter-Korean relations or unification. As the peninsula moves toward unification, or at least sweeping change in North Korea, the strategic equilibrium on the peninsula will break up. In addition to transforming the Korean peninsula itself, Korean unification could lead to a partial or total withdrawal of U.S. forces from Northeast Asia. This report will analyze the implications of change on the Korean peninsula for regional security. It will conclude by making the case that a U.S. military disengagement from Northeast Asia would lead to regional instability and that developments in the region call for strengthening rather than weakening U.S. military ties with the Republic of Korea and Japan and for the continued deployment of American ground forces in both countries after Korean unification.

Northeast Asia is a sharply bifurcated region, one part wealthy and capitalist, the other one poor and either communist or in transition from Marxism. Rich Northeast Asia comprises South Korea, Japan, and Taiwan. With over $5.5 trillion of GDP (mostly in Japan), Northeast Asia is one of the three pillars of the world economy. Moreover, these capitalist nations fuel Chinese and Southeast Asian growth, thanks to trade and investment. Commerce with capitalist Northeast Asia, and other East Asian nations, enriches the United States and is essential to America's global role. Over 20 percent of American trade is with Northeast Asia, and without strong ties with that region American economic well-being and security would be gravely endangered.

China, North Korea, and the Russian Far East are the other part of Northeast Asia. They are not rich market economies but belong to the Northeast Asian strategic region because of the linkages which bind them to each other and to South Korea, Japan, and Taiwan. China has important economic links with Japan and South Korea, as does the Russian Far East. North Korea is the northern half of the divided Korea. China considers Taiwan a part of the country, and there are major commercial and business connections across the Taiwan Strait in spite of political hostility. Therefore, the two Koreas, Japan, China, Taiwan, and Far Eastern Russia form a single strategic region. This makes it impossible to analyze the security dilemmas facing Korea without including all of Northeast Asia. The United States, because of its military and economic role in East Asia, is a major component of the regional strategic equation, and the United States is thus an extraterritorial member of Northeast Asia.

In the past decades Northeast Asia has been stable. In the coming years, however, upheavals on the Korean peninsula might spark a chain reaction, starting with an American withdrawal from Asia and ending in vicious rivalries involving Korea, Japan, China, Taiwan, and perhaps Russia, which could wreck the regional order and end both peace and prosperity. The technological, financial, and human resources of Northeast Asia are enormous. An unstable security environment could ignite conflicts of a cataclysmic magnitude because the nations of Northeast Asia, unlike those of the Caucasus and the Balkans, are neither poor nor small. Thanks to their wealth and population, Northeast Asian states could bring to the battlefield awesome quantities of firepower and soldiers, even if there is no foreign intervention.

Korea is the key to Northeast Asia's security because the arrangements resulting from the Korean War are the core of the strategic architecture which keeps the peace in the region. The key feature of this environment is a *pax americana*, guaranteed by an American military deployment in Korea and reinforced by strong U.S. ground, air, and naval units in Japan. Besides protecting South Korea and Japan, the United States also contributes to the defense of Taiwan. Moreover, America attenuates the lingering suspicions which Asian states hold against one another because the U.S. military presence makes it less likely that any Asian power can successfully alter the regional balance of power or local borders.

These post-Korean War arrangements may soon be altered abruptly because the Korean peninsula is on the brink of a major upheaval. North Korea, of doubtful stability since the USSR ceased supporting it and Kim Il Sung died, may soon undergo radical change or implode. It is not our purpose, however, to predict the course of North Korean developments but to lay out some of the issues which will arise as a result of the changes which are likely to occur as a result of developments in North Korea. The major factors which lead us to think that North Korea's regime will vanish or undergo a metamorphosis are as follows:

1. The death of the founder of the state and his replacement by an untested successor has undermined the regime. Kim's DPRK was communist, but the legitimacy of the system relied more on a single charismatic god-like leader than any other Marxist-Leninist nation (even Stalin never resorted to the same "cult of personality" as Kim Il Sung). The high-profile defections which have occurred since his demise are an indicator of the impact of his death. The regime is therefore less secure without Kim Il Sung, and the chances of an overthrow of the dynasty are higher.

2. The end of the Soviet Union has terminated Soviet support for the North Korean state. It has removed from the scene the only country which had the power to veto, if it wanted, any arrangement which might have endangered Pyongyang's survival. As long as the Soviet Union existed and there was a Cold War between Moscow and Washington, the North Korean regime enjoyed superpower protection.

3. Events in former communist nations have demonstrated that party officials can thrive after communism if they manage the transition well (e.g., Yeltsin, Karimov, Nyazov, and thousands of beneficiaries of "*nomenklatura* privatizations"). On the other hand, communist rulers can lose their lives (Ceaucescu, Najibulah) or be forced into exile (Hoenecker) if they play their cards badly. This should motivate members of the ruling circles to take the initiative to shape a new North Korea rather than be the victims of history.

4. The economic and agricultural crisis could induce some factions of the ruling class to alter the entire economic system. North Korea's *nomenklatura* may not care about the fate of the people, but at some point economic failure will affect the elite's standard of living and its ability to keep the state apparatus in working order. The Chinese example is another demonstration (at least so far) that it is possible for communist parties to undertake economic reform while maintaining political power. Therefore, some elements within the ruling party in North Korea might pursue a Chinese road. This could start a process which over the next ten years could transform North Korea.

5. China has established strong ties with South Korea and

curtailed its subsidies to the North. As a consequence, North Korea is now left without any powerful sponsor. The United States is now the most important foreign power for North Korea because it can provide a diplomatic and economic lifeboat for the regime. Establishing good relations with the U.S. would, however, probably entail internal changes. The desire to attract foreign investment to surmount economic difficulties could also force changes upon the regime.

6. The South is wary of the costs of rapid unification; its preferred option is to seek slow, gradual, and positive changes in its relations with the North. This may lead some Northern leaders to hope that they can reach a *modus vivendi* with Seoul because their services will be useful in what South Korea hopes will be a very long transition period. Therefore, the Northern rulers might hope to preside over major reforms and keep their positions with Seoul's approval.

7. Finally, in the past years, a few members of the North Korean elite have traveled to the capitalist world, including South Korea. Regardless of their ideological indoctrination, they must have awakened to the abysmal failure of their system, and their self-confidence must have been shaken.

In light of these circumstances, there are three possible scenarios for the evolution of the situation on the Korean peninsula over the coming years.

The first scenario is that Korea will remain divided but that systemic change will occur in the North. For example, North Korea could adopt a Chinese system, mixing political dictatorship (though not of the totalitarian Kim Il Sung variety), a semi-market economy, and foreign investment in selected zones. These changes would not propel the North to prosperity on the South Korean scale, but they could save the regime for several years from imploding by bringing in foreign exchange and saving the economy from total bankruptcy. Such reforms could be accompanied by disarmament and confidence-building measures to pave the way to reduction of tensions, the dismantlement of the DMZ, and the establishment of peaceful relations between the two Koreas. The model for such relations could be Sino-Taiwanese relations when Beijing is in a tolerant phase. In the long run, such a compromise could lead either unification or, less probably, the establishment of two separate Korean-speaking states enjoying good relations (on the model of Austro-German or U.S.-Canadian ties, for example).

The second option, after a transitional phase or a breakdown of the northern dictatorship, is the complete unification of the country under the government of the Republic of Korea. If North Koreans feel more "Korean" than "North Korean," a political crisis or coup could degenerate into irrepressible calls for the unification of the motherland. Under the impulse of nationalism, the Northern government could lose control of gradual reforms while citizens on both sides of the DMZ would press for unification. Seoul opposes a quick merger; but unification has been its stated goal since the founding of the Republic. Consequently, if there is a collapse of order in North Korea accompanied by nationalist calls for unification in both Korean states, it will be most difficult for the ROK government to avoid having to merge the northern provinces into the Republic.

The third possibility is that the Korean peninsula will remain unchanged. Under such circumstances, the DRPK would survive unreformed, and the armed truce which has prevailed since 1953 would continue. Though Pyongyang may be more resilient than expected, it is very doubtful that in 2008 the North Korean regime will still be the same as in 1998.

The first two scenarios, which together are far more likely than the third, will spur a diplomatic revolution in Northeast Asia. Division, and subsequent intractable tensions, have defined Korean internal and foreign policies since 1953. Unification, or a peaceful settlement of the North-South dispute, will open new vistas for Korea. As chapter 2 explains, Korea will face great opportunities—but also many challenges—in the wake of the end of a peace settlement or unification.

Chapter 3 looks at Korean unification and Asian security from Japan's point of view. Japan is ill-equipped to deal with a post-unification Asia which did not include a continued massive U.S. military commitment to the region, and therefore Korean unification could be the greatest challenge to Japan's national security since the end of the Occupation.

Developments in Korea will also affect China, which shares a long border with North Korea. North Korea's existence has allowed China to benefit from economic intercourse with South Korea while keeping the North Korean buffer between South Korea (and the U.S. army) and the People's Republic. Unification will lead to the establishment of a border between the Republic of Korea and the PRC. Disputes over the presence of American soldiers in Korea, and over the relationship between ethnic Koreans in China and Korea, could embroil Beijing in confrontations with Seoul and Washington. China might also be emboldened by Korean unification to seek its own "unification" with Taiwan, thereby risking a violent confrontation with America. Chapter 4 will review China's stake in developments in Korea and the implications for the region.

Though weakened, Russia remains a significant player in Asia and plays a role in regional security. Chapter 5 will explain how Russia's policy in Asia has vacillated between different goals, and why Moscow should not be forgotten when analyzing Asia's strategic balance.

Chapter 6 concludes this study by looking at the implications of these issues for American policy and offers ideas for an American strategy in the post-unification era.

Chapter Two
Korea[*]

Identification of the Problem

The Republic of Korea (ROK) has undergone a perennial anguish in assessing the security situation on the Korean peninsula, its focus being always on the North Korean military threat. While a hostile North Korea remains the most serious danger to the South's national integrity and likely will continue to be so for the foreseeable future, the probability of the former's imminent collapse, either through implosion or explosion, only adds difficulties to the deliberations of ROK defense planners. Moreover, whether the collapse of the Kim Jong-il regime will mean the collapse of the socialist system, the state itself, or whether both will be followed by an interim regime is another source of uncertainty and controversy. Because of the uncertain nature of the danger posed by the highly unpredictable North, implementing a short-term defense policy has, clearly, become a difficult matter for the ROK Ministry of National Defense.

Obviously, the security environment of the Korean peninsula around the year 2010, the hypothetical year of Korean unification laid out in this chapter, will be forged by many factors. The future of North Korea, for example, constitutes the major deciding factor for peace and unification of Korea. If the current North Korean regime collapses from an implosion within two or three years as many in the United States have predicted, the handling of the post-Kim Jong-il North Korea would be a tremendous burden for the ROK. And the competition for potential influence over post-unification Korea would be fierce among the regional powers. On the other hand, if a desperate North Korea explodes—that is, launches a war against the South, as a means to overcome its internal crisis—the entire Korean peninsula will once again

[*] The author is writing in his personal capacity and the opinions expressed in this chapter do not necessarily reflect the views of the Korea Institute for Defense Analyses, the Ministry of National Defense of the Republic of Korea, or the Government of the Republic of Korea.

suffer insurmountable calamities. Even though the combined forces of the ROK and the U.S. will win the war, other countries in the region may well intervene in one way or another, making a postwar phase more complex than otherwise anticipated. If somehow North Korea avoids both scenarios, muddles through the current crisis, succeeds in normalizing its relations with the United States and Japan, and makes substantial progress in North-South dialogues, it will pave the way for its economic recovery and a prolonged existence. In this case, the surrounding countries would most likely uphold the status quo.

To be sure, the Korean problem is extremely difficult to diagnose and even more difficult to prescribe. And further compounding questions abound. How long will the Kim Jong-il regime last without giving up its hostile policy toward the South? What if, after Pyongyang survives current regime-threatening difficulties and enters a reconciliation phase with Seoul, the North Korean threat declines significantly and eventually disappears? And what if the two Koreas are finally unified? What would be the roles of the neighboring countries in the process of unification? Once unification is achieved or imminent, what change would then occur in the newly unified Korea's perception of threat—one that has long been focused on the North? How would its neighbors react to this monumental change on the Korean peninsula? These are some of the questions that have emerged since the death of Kim Il Sung in 1994.

The answers to these questions will be quite complicated, perhaps beyond our best imagination. The future of North Korea is fairly uncertain for the next two or three years, and is extremely uncertain for the years thereafter. Indeed, for the past forty-five years since the end of the Korean War, ROK security policy and the combined ROK-U.S. military command and force structure have centered on the North Korean threat, both real and imagined. However, as Seoul and Washington endeavor to induce a soft landing for the Pyongyang regime, even as they remain equally apprehensive of an imminent collapse that will bring about devastation, defense planners in both capitals are making efforts to reflect these changes in making their defense policies. Likewise, some intellectuals and government officials in the ROK and the United States seem to be paying renewed attention to how the ROK-U.S. alliance in general, and the U.S. military presence in Korea in particular, will evolve. Even the prospect of a unified Korea will prompt the ROK government to take a new look at the rules of the game and new thinking about external threats and ways to counter them effectively. Finally, how a unified Korea would perceive its external threats will have no small impact on Northeast Asia's security environment.

It goes without saying that the security environment of a unified Korea will be forged by many factors, including developments in South and North Korea, the North-South Korean relationship, the roles of the surrounding powers, and the relations among these powers. To be more specific, the future of North Korea, the North-South Korean relationship, the process leading to unification, and the roles of neighboring countries in contingencies as well as in the peace process will significantly affect the security environment of a unified Korea. Also, the unification process, and the timing and modality of Korean unification, will have a profound impact on the security environment in Northeast Asia around 2010.

In other words, sudden collapse of the North Korean regime, followed by its absorption by South Korea, would be a quite different scenario from the protracted case of a gradual unification through exchanges, cooperation, and integration of the two Koreas.[1] The disappearance of the current North Korean regime, or the state itself, in a relatively short period of time would probably cause a strategic vacuum, in reaction to which South Korea and the surrounding powers would hurriedly contend to protect their national interests, with some unexpected clashes. This would be particularly true as long as Beijing views Washington and Tokyo as trying to infringe upon what it perceives as its intrinsic rights in the region. Conversely, if North Korea successfully negotiates with Seoul, and comes to normal terms with South Korea, neighboring countries would have enough time and latitude to adjust themselves to a prospective unification of the two Koreas and the ensuing changes in the strategic landscape of Northeast Asia.

Thus this chapter will explore the factors that will have a decisive impact on the peace and unification of Korea, including those of the two Koreas, their relations, the roles of the neighboring powers, and finally the security environment of a unified Korea. The assumption is that over the next ten to fifteen years, the Korean situation will be profoundly altered, either by a radical change in inter-Korean relations or by unification. Externally, major powers, particularly the United States and China, will play decisive roles in bringing peace and unification to the Korean peninsula. One of the major implications of these domestic and foreign factors is that as the strategic equilibrium changes fundamentally, we will witness an increasing demand for partial or total withdrawal of U.S. troops from Northeast Asia. Additionally, changing strategic relationships among the regional powers will result in new roles and missions for

the militaries of countries in the region. The U.S. defense commitment, in the form of forward deployment and projection of power
from afar, will nevertheless continue for reasons other than those
that existed during the Cold War era. The driving force behind this
is an uncertain dynamism that will continue to be a dominating char-
acteristic of the Northeast Asian landscape even after the unification of the two Koreas.

DEVELOPMENTS IN SOUTH KOREA
Conflicting Views on North Korea

In a pluralistic society like today's South Korea, there are numerous divergent and competing views on many issues. Issues such as the
North Korean threat, the likelihood of an immediate collapse of North
Korea, and the timing and formula of unification are no exception.
Competing views in South Korea have apparently been influenced by
many recent developments in North Korea, such as the vacancy in the
presidency since the death of Kim Il Sung, severe food shortages, and
an ever-increasing number of defectors, both civilians and government
officials. To some, these are the signs of a reduced threat and the imminent collapse of the Kim Jong-il regime and quite possibly the state
of North Korea itself, thus shortening the process of unification. To
others, these do not have much to do with an impending collapse or a
declining threat from North Korea. Instead, they believe that the North
Korean threat is real, that the current North Korean regime is solid
enough to overcome the current crisis, and that it will survive for many
more years to come.

Similarly, views on contingencies in North Korea, and responses
by South Korea and its neighbors also differ markedly. Many believe
that because any serious contingency will mean the end of the Kim
Jong-il regime and the state of North Korea, South Korea should oppose any foreign intervention and take advantage of the opportunity to
unify the North and South. Others believe that any serious contingency
will be met with serious intervention by major powers, thus restricting
the freedom of the ROK, and will possibly prolong the process of unification. In other words, the internationalization of peace and unification on the Korean peninsula appears almost unavoidable to these
pessimists.

Opinions also differ widely regarding the unification formula and
its cost. At the risk of over-generalization, one school of thought prefers a swift absorption of the North by the South, following the collapse
of the North Korean regime, before the situation becomes more

complicated as the result of the intervention of neighboring countries. They argue that this swiftness can diminish the cost of both division and unification. Another school of thought prefers unification by agreement and believes South Koreans cannot afford the cost of unification because of current economic difficulties. They suggest instead that South Korea help North Korea stand on its own feet, thereby facilitating a peaceful unification through mutual agreement by the two Koreas. These individuals, who are increasing in number especially among young generations, are thus questioning the rationale for unification.

Policy Toward North Korea

Because of these widely diverging assessments and views on the present and future of North Korea, making policy toward North Korea has not been an easy job. In fact, some have openly criticized South Korea's policy toward North Korea as being adrift. Even though the basic modality of North-South relations was laid out in the 1991 Basic Agreement and the Korean National Community unification formula, there have been some lingering perceptions that the ROK's policy has not been very effective. There has been a widely shared consensus among these differing South Koreans, however, on the need to deter a war (and, if deterrence fails, to win it rapidly) and the need to achieve a peaceful unification as opposed to unification by force.

Assuming that the North Korean regime will not collapse in the near future but will do so eventually, there are basically two options for ROK policy toward North Korea. (The first is to help the North reform and open its society, the so-called sunshine theory. The second is to contain it and push it toward further isolation and surrender, the so-called wind theory.[2]) The former theory has it that only the sunshine, not the wind, can open North Korean society. Some people such as the senior North Korean official, Hwang Jang-yop, who recently defected, however, fear that the former policy will only help justify the Kim Jong-il regime by saving its economy and that the South will in the long run confront an even stronger and more intransigent enemy in the North. Consequently, they argue that the chance for unification will be further delayed. In this context, those who opt for a tough policy of containment and strangulation of the North Korean regime believe that it will eventually quicken the timing of unification and lower the overall cost of unification.

On the defense side, ROK defense policy for many decades has been composed of three key elements: deterrence and defense against North Korea's military threat, alliance with the United Sates, and security cooperation with a group of other countries. It is quite fair to say that North Korea is a state that defies common-sense explanation and understanding. It is extremely difficult to know what is happening in the inner sanctum of the Pyongyang regime, despite highly sophisticated intelligence gathering devices flying near and over North Korean territory. The country's external policy appears sometimes rational, sometimes irrational. It has been known as a rogue state, because of the pattern of unexpected attitudes and behavior it has shown in its dealings with the outside world. Faced with the military threat of this rogue state, ROK defense policy has had to deal with the dual task of countering North Korea's real military threat and adjusting to changes in the security environment in Northeast Asia.

The disappearance of the North Korean military threat, or at least the perception of its disappearance, and the timing and modality of unification will heavily influence ROK defense policy toward North Korea. The basic assumption in ROK defense policy planning has been that North Korea's military threat will gradually decline but remain meaningful for several years, and that a complete unification of the two Koreas will not come until at least the turn of the century. At the same time, contingency planning has been given rekindled attention recently because of the looming possibility of the collapse of the current Pyongyang regime in the near future.[3] This contingency planning, in conjunction with the U.S.-Japan guidelines for defense cooperation, will likely dominate South Korean discussions as long as North Korea suffers from severe food shortages and political instability. Accordingly, ROK defense policy aims to be flexible and adaptive enough to counter any contingency in North Korea. On the other hand, it aims at staving off these contingencies in North Korea and inducing openness and reform there.

Nevertheless, scenarios of an imminent collapse of North Korea may have the merit of alerting the ROK political leadership. Such scenarios, unwittingly stimulate the false hope of an absorption-type unification on South Korea's own terms in the near future, and make one suspicious of the utility of the costly soft-landing approach that the U.S. and the ROK have adopted in recent years. This in turn appears to have caused a seemingly intensified Seoul-Washington friction over their policy coordination.[4] Furthermore, ROK defense policy designed for the post-North Korean threat has unnecessarily incurred suspicion and worry on the part of neighboring countries, especially Japan.

At least for the next two to three years, as the absolute gap in the national power of the North and South widens, North Korea's sense of inferiority and crisis will intensify. This situation in turn may explain the North Koreans' refusal to talk with South Korea. North Korea's regime may well continue to stress its survival, need for deterrence, and self-protection, while sticking to its policy of brinkmanship tactics and military provocations. It is ironic that North Korea's weakness has now become its strength. It follows, therefore, that as long as Pyongyang refuses to show its willingness to live in peace with South Korea and to open meaningful discussions, the latter's defense policy will basically remain the same.

However, once the situation in North Korea is fundamentally altered—through either collapse or unification—ROK defense policy will also change. If the current regime collapses via a palace coup or mass revolt and is succeeded by a technocrat-ruled interim regime, the ROK will pursue various CBMs and arms control measures with the North. This accommodating defense policy will then give more weight to extensive military cooperation with the neighboring powers. The ROK-U.S. command relationship will begin to evolve significantly to reflect these fundamental changes in the North-South Korean relationship. Also, multilateral security forums will be convened to discuss the entire Korean situation.

If the current regime in Pyongyang manages its crisis and the two Koreas are eventually united by agreement following the phase of reconciliation and harmony and the phase of integration, the ROK will have adjusted its defense policy accordingly. While maintaining its alliance with the United States, it will actively pursue multilateral security dialogues and cooperation with all the neighbors, as a means of complementing the bilateral relationship. Its relations with its neighbors will fundamentally change, and it will be assiduously engaged in building regional collective security arrangements.

The Domestic Situation

The ROK has its own political and economic problems to resolve. After achieving the remarkable combination of a peaceful transition to political democracy and economic growth, a host of problems that often emerge in the process of systemic adjustment have surfaced. In fact, South Korea has its own economic vulnerabilities, due largely to the "bubbles" of a high-rate economic growth. These systemic problems, represented by prohibitively high real estate and housing prices, weakened industrial competitiveness, and growing current account and trade deficits have recently produced a sense of an impending economic and financial crisis. This crisis, if it continues, will have substantial impact on the North-South relationship. For example, the impact of providing assistance to North Korea would be great and taxpayers would feel increasingly burdened by various projects that are underway or will begin in North Korea.

Humanitarian food assistance to North Korea is an example of this issue. In a humanitarian gesture the ROK government provided 150,000 tons of rice to North Korea in 1995. In local elections that year, the ruling party suffered heavy losses. Because of the flagging and espionage incidents during the summer, public opinion turned against assisting North Korea.[5] This is a prime example of how domestic politics can easily mix with the economy in inter-Korean relations. Besides, the lack of proper means to check on whether or not the food provided is diverted to military use causes grave concern and reservation among policymakers and the general public alike.

Funding unification will also be a critical issue facing the ROK's government. For one thing, South Korea's share of KEDO (Korean Peninsula Energy Development Organization) expenses will be politically problematic, especially if the ROK's economic slump lasts longer than expected. As a matter of fact, the plans to construct two LWRs (Light Water Reactors) have been protracted, and the estimated cost has risen markedly to some $7 billion. South Korea will thus need to pick up a much larger tab, and the remaining portion of the bill will be negotiated among KEDO participants. In a similar manner, outsourcing needs to be given serious thought in preparing the unification fund.

In addition, the results of the upcoming presidential elections in December 1997 will affect Seoul's mid- to long-term policy toward Pyongyang. Even if all the presidential candidates are supportive of improving relations with the North, they can be divided into moderates and progressives. If a progressive gets elected, ROK policy will probably be more forthcoming and accommodating to North Korea. Likewise, in the general elections, local elections, and presidential elections to be held until 2010, post-Korean War generations will occupy most of the important posts in the government. To maximize the national interest, the people will pursue exchanges and cooperation with North Korea on an extensive level, and make efforts to integrate and unify the long-separated North and South. Additionally, local autonomy will be increasingly vocal and visible in the years to come, with some tangible impact on many issues related to peace and unification.

DEVELOPMENTS IN NORTH KOREA

North Korea's regime has firmly defended itself, despite the decline of socialism on the world scene. Its current regime holds fast to the aged *Juche* (self-reliance) ideology and "Red Banner" ideas to solidify its socialist system. Thus, it seems quite unlikely that the Kim Jong-il regime will opt for openness and reforms in the near future—an indication that the future is not bright for poverty-stricken, diplomatically-isolated North Korea. Quite naturally, most North Korea watchers are concerned about the length of time it will take for the North to collapse, whether it is capable of managing crises, whether it intends to open and reform, and how serious these intentions are. Developments in North Korea in the next ten years or so are almost impossible to predict with any accuracy. But one can postulate three most probable scenarios—survival of the current Kim Jong-il regime (gradual decline), his resignation and the collapse of his regime (sudden collapse), and stability and development of the North Korean regime (crisis overcome).

The Likelihood of Collapse

In predicting the future of North Korea, the dominant concern in recent years has been the prospect of a collapse of the current North Korean regime. This was apparently prompted by a growing number of North Korean refugees and defectors, severe shortages of food and energy, and continued economic decline. These grim scenes have led many to speculate on the future course of North Korea in a pessimistic way, the so-called hard-landing, or as Stanley Roth has put it, a softer hard-landing.[6] On the other hand, there have been also predictions for a longer-than-expected durability of the North Korean regime despite these hardships, notably among South Korean defense experts. These opinions have been echoed by many Japanese, Chinese, and Russian experts on Korean affairs, who, unlike their American counterparts, have a much more positive view of the sustainability of the North Korean regime.[7]

Similarly, before Kim Il Sung died, many observers in South Korea and other countries predicted that his death would bring about fundamental changes in North Korean politics and the North-South relationship, and perhaps quicken the process of unification. No such changes have occurred so far in the North, and the North-South relationship remains basically unchanged. Without officially assuming the presidency, the junior Kim has ruled the country for three years since the death of his father in the name of following his father's legacy, which has been sarcastically called "the politics of a ghost." All these conflicting views and predictions suggest the extreme difficulty of fore-telling the future of the Kim Jong-il regime and the state of North Korea.[8] What, then, is the likelihood of the collapse of the Pyongyang regime?

With no imminent signs of reform or openness in the North Korean leadership, coupled with a growing number of high-ranking govern-ment officials defecting to the South, a basket-case economy, and highly visible media reports of malnutrition and starvation, the North Korean regime is in an unprecedented crisis. But is it actually on the verge of collapse, as many people would like to believe? The North Korean regime may go in the direction of collapse, unless it introduces reform measures and is aided by South Korea and the surrounding powers.[9] Here, the problem is with the assumptions. Unlike some Eastern Euro-pean countries that witnessed the ouster of their communist dictators and the collapse of their regimes, China and Vietnam have gradually introduced economic openness and some political reforms while main-taining the outer shell of socialism. Moreover, many Asian countries have survived severe food shortages and mass starvation, as in the case of Imperial Japan during World War II and Communist China under Mao. Also, neighboring countries would quite likely help North Korea to prevent it from collapsing. Chances are thus as good for the survival as for the collapse of the Pyongyang regime.

While there are many external factors that can help delay or deter the collapse, the general mood until quite recently has been closer to the unavoidability of collapse and how to minimize the impact.[10] As a result, North Korean contingencies have become the subject of pri-mary concern and hot debates in neighboring countries. The United States has been particularly concerned with these contingencies and how to deal effectively with them in cooperation with the ROK and Japan. The revision of the Guidelines for U.S.-Japan Defense Coop-eration is a prime example of how much attention the two countries are paying to this issue. Not only the ROK and the U.S., Japan and China, but also, though to a lesser degree, other countries such as Rus-sia, Australia, and Canada, have shown keen interest in developments in North Korea.

On the other hand, as the United States began to engage North Korea in its diplomatic talks, an increasing number of North Korea experts concur with a different three-phase scenario, which has been the official view of the ROK government and is shared by a KIDA-RAND joint study.[11] Similar findings were reached in a survey

conducted for the Advisory Council for Democracy and Peaceful Unification, a blue-ribbon policy advisory group. Some 80 percent of the
respondents said that the Pyongyang regime would not collapse but
rather sustain itself.[12] Likewise, the basic assumption of this chapter is
that the two Koreas will likely be unified by the year 2010 following
the second phase of exchanges, cooperation and integration, as different from scenarios of a sudden collapse of the Kim Jong-il regime or
of the succeeding ruling groups. This does not mean, however, that the
ROK can afford not to make preparations for unforeseen events taking
place in North Korea.

Relations with the United States

Another basic premise of this chapter is that major powers surrounding the Korean peninsula can and should help construct the peace
regime in Korea.[13] Pyongyang's approach to Washington at the expense of Seoul has been taken almost for granted during the past several years. Ironically, Pyongyang needs a helping hand from its long-
time arch-enemy, the United States, to guarantee that the regime will
survive. It has already embarked on serious talks with Washington on
some pending issues, including the Four-party Talks, the search and
return of the remains of American POWs and MIAs during the Korean War, and North Korea's missile exports. Thus far the United States
has sent many teams of former and current high-ranking government
officials and influential congressmen to discuss, for example, food provision, the easing and lifting of economic sanctions, trade and investment, the Four-party Talks, and other issues related to improving
relations.

The leadership in Pyongyang will most likely seek to follow the
pattern of the Hanoi-Washington normalization process. Former ad-
versaries, Vietnam and the United States finally exchanged ambassa-
dors in 1995. Trade has since increased between the two countries,
and, in spite of the problems due to the collapse of the USSR, Vietnam's
regime has kept its independence and achieved economic growth. It
joined ASEAN in 1996, and seeks to engage in many other multilateral
forums. It appears that North Korea has actually taken similar steps in
pursuit of normalizing relations with the United States. Bilateral talks
have progressed at a substantial level, and the Four-party Talks will be
held soon. Many steps still have to be taken before their normalization,
however, including excavating crash sites and common burial sites for
the remains of U.S. POWs and MIAs, lifting economic sanctions, opening liaison offices, and visits of high-ranking officials.

In the near term, Pyongyang will continue to underscore the importance of concluding a separate peace treaty with Washington, which it believes will guarantee its political legitimacy and independence. It will also accept and even praise the United States' leading role in maintaining the status quo on the Korean peninsula, and will utilize its improving relations with Washington to solicit support from neighboring countries, most notably Japan. In the meantime, Pyongyang will continue to seek to trade its acceptance of the USFK in exchange for normal relations with the U.S.

NORTH-SOUTH KOREAN RELATIONS

Fearing eventual absorption by the South and with a sense of inferiority vis-à-vis the South, North Korea has recently been adamantly opposed to resuming any official dialogue with Seoul. The Pyongyang regime has not abandoned its long-held policy of unifying the Korean peninsula on its terms (the only rationale for its authoritarian dictatorship). The Pyongyang "Garrison State" hopes to accomplish this by continuous military buildups and excruciating sacrifices forced on its people. Because the regime in Pyongyang faces multiple threats and dangers, it wishes to pursue diplomatic normalization with and economic assistance from the United States and Japan, its traditional enemies, while bypassing South Korea.

In a sense, the future of North Korea depends heavily on the policy of South Korea towards the North. If the latter chooses to assist the former seriously in its soft-line policy, a favorable atmosphere will be created among the regional powers to help an ailing North Korea. It will require confidence and patience to do that. Once Pyongyang recovers from its desperate preoccupation with the choice of collapse or survival, it will in all probability come to the negotiating table. By then, there will be a new government in Seoul, and chances are that the North Korean leadership will be stabilized. Also, as Pyongyang becomes more confident and succeeds in its economic reforms, economic and social-cultural exchanges and cooperation will be actively implemented between the North and South. The groundwork for these extended interactions of the two Koreas has already been laid in the North-South Basic Agreement on Reconciliation, Non-intervention and Exchanges and Cooperation, signed in December 1991, and the Joint Declaration on the Denuclearization of the Korean Peninsula signed in January 1992.

As an example of these interactions, the KEDO Project to build two LWRs in the remote town of Sinpo in North Korea is scheduled for completion by 2005. The ROK will play the central role and pay the largest portion of the costs. The implementation of the project will likely help North Korea survive. A mini-Marshall plan might be pursued to restore the economy of North Korea. In the meantime, ROK investment and business activities will continue to expand in the Rajin-Sonbong Free Trade Zone and others. These growing interactions between the two Koreas and other major powers will facilitate a variety of confidence-building measures between the two Koreas. Multilateral security forums charged with tackling the North Korean problem will thrive. All this may sound far too optimistic, but it can be realized if all countries in the region agree on this course of action for North Korea. And they have good reason to do so.

In recent years there has been a tendency in South Korea to conceptualize ROK-U.S. and U.S.-DPRK relations as a zero-sum game, with any improvement in relations between Washington and Pyongyang being a loss for Seoul. A growing number of people, both experts and ordinary citizens, look at the security relationship between Seoul and Washington through the lens of the burgeoning Washington-Pyongyang one. Moreover, some observers have now begun to see the Seoul-Washington security relationship through yet another lens, the disappointingly stalled Seoul-Pyongyang relationship. There has been a widespread perception among South Koreans that their country was left isolated or marginalized in the negotiating process prior to the signing of the October 1994 Geneva Agreed Framework, which was designed primarily to freeze Pyongyang's suspected nuclear development program and for normalizing relations between Washington and Pyongyang. This perception has been joined by other perceptions that perceive Seoul's policy toward Pyongyang has been drifting and that there have been growing ROK-U.S. conflicts over North Korea policy. There have been increasing reports of conflicts in ROK-U.S. relations vis-à-vis North Korea. In particular, the often-quoted initial response by then U.S. Secretary of State Warren Christopher at the time of a North Korean submarine incursion in September 1996 enhanced these perceptions.

Once these perceptions disappear, however, North-South relations will enter a new phase. This will be possible, in fact, only when the Pyongyang regime restores self-confidence and frees itself from the fear of collapse and absorption by the South. At this stage, the inter-Korean relationship will benefit from exchanges and cooperation in many fields.

ROLES OF NEIGHBORING POWERS

This section addresses the position of neighboring countries in the unification process. Of these neighboring countries, which countries will support or detract from the unification of North and South Korea? Under which circumstances will they make such decisions?[14]

Many Koreans used to place greater importance on external factors rather than on domestic Korean factors. This tendency has markedly weakened, and many Koreans now believe that they can play a central role and that their own contributions can affect those of the neighboring powers. Undoubtedly the majority of Koreans today have a strong desire for eventual unification without outside intervention. They have a strong sense of independence and self-sufficiency, free from the two geographically close and historically harassing powers of Japan and China. Nevertheless, neighboring powers will have a significant impact on any future peace regime and the timing and modality of Korean unification.

In the years up to 2010, Korea, united or not, will likely remain inferior to all of its neighboring countries in national power including military power. China, with its sustained economic growth and as "potential theater-peer competitor," will likely challenge the United States and Japan in their pursuit of a favorable strategic environment.[15] Japan, for all its domestic political problems and challenges from abroad, will probably maintain an economic and technological edge and play an extended security role. Russia will regain its strength, at least to some extent, as its political and economic difficulties are resolved. The United States is likely to maintain its military presence at a somewhat reduced level and yet continue to exert powerful influence in regional security. Positioned next to these four superpowers, a unified Korea will likely confront a broad array of threats and dangers arising from various sources.

The question, then, is whether or not history will repeat itself in this part of the world. In the late nineteenth century, the Korean peninsula was the arena where the interests of the four surrounding powers intersected. Can one make the same historical analogy for post-unification Korea? In the strict sense of the term, history does not repeat itself. Only perceptions do.[16] Still, history often gives similar lessons to students of a succeeding generation. As many historians agree, the past does help put present phenomena in perspective. If one can learn any lesson from history, the primary mission of the unified Korea should be to prevent similar historical incidents from happening again.

The Role of the United States

Many indicators show that the United States will continue to be the predominant power well into the twenty-first century. With its economy stable and growing again after many years of economic slump, the United States, as the only remaining superpower on the globe, appears to have the power to "lead" the world. The debate over the "relative declinism" of the United States seems to have dissipated in favor of U.S. "leadership." In the early 1990s the prevailing perception among Asian countries was that a declining U.S. would have to withdraw from East Asia. An ever-growing China, it was thought, would fill the strategic vacuum, and, consequently, the security situation would be further destabilized by arms races among the regional powers. To stave off this worry, the Clinton Administration declared in its 1994 *East Asia Strategic Review* its intent to station some 100,000 troops in East Asia for the foreseeable future. The importance of the Korean peninsula in U.S. military strategy was manifested in the so-called win-win strategy, which was retained in the recently published *Report of the Quadrennial Defense Review*. In fact, there are no indications that the USFK will withdraw from the Korean peninsula in the near future.

The national strategy of cooperative engagement will continue to allow the United States to play an important role in insuring peace and prosperity in Northeast Asia. Now with direct talks with an eager North Korea on many issues (including a new peace regime and diplomatic normalization), and with a forward military presence in East Asia, the United States can and will make the greatest contributions to the peace and unification of Korea. Of the four major powers around the Korean peninsula, it seems most likely that the United States will play the most important role in bringing positive changes to the Korean peninsula. It has the power, experience, and will, to play an arbitrator role, while making the most of its vested interests in Korea.[17]

In the short term, the U.S. can be instrumental in deterring another war by maintaining a strong combined defense readiness with the ROK Armed Forces while standing pat on its policy of upholding the existing Armistice Agreement, in close consultation with the ROK. Equally important, it can contribute to a new peace regime in Korea by fully implementing its 1994 Geneva Agreed Framework and by actively engaging in the Four-party Talks, both of which are designed to help put Pyongyang on the road to economic recovery, limited liberalization, and political reforms. Washington, in close consultation with Seoul, will provide Pyongyang with a detailed roadmap for its soft-landing in order to build a firm peace regime on the Korean peninsula.

In addition to deterring and defending against North Korea's war machine, the United States can play a much-needed role in dealing with unforeseen contingencies coming from North Korea that could spill over into the neighboring countries.[18] To be more specific, Washington can consult with Seoul on how to deal with major emergencies in North Korea—their respective roles, joint roles, UN roles, etc. in each of the most probable contingency scenarios. Part of this contingency is likely to be quietly pursued in discussions with Japan and, to a lesser extent, China, who were in one way or another involved in the division of Korea and the Korean War. In short, the United States would try to move "beyond deterrence" to ready itself for any contingencies in North Korea and/or to induce a soft-landing in North Korea despite the pessimistic predictions many analysts have made.[19]

U.S. efforts to engage North Korea in order to reduce tension on the Korean peninsula will be tested at the Four-party Talks proposed jointly by Presidents Kim and Clinton in April 1996, as will the implementation of the 1994 Geneva Agreed Framework to freeze North Korea's nuclear weapons program. KEDO has already begun construction work on the two LWRs in Sinpo, North Korea. Other channels of negotiation with Pyongyang—talks regarding the provision of food and heavy oil, counter-proliferation of North Korean missiles and weapons of mass destruction, return of MIA/POW remains, easing of economic sanctions—can facilitate confidence building between the United States and DPRK.[20] If some of these talks turn out to be successful for both countries in the near future, they will set the stage for a normal relationship. All the other talks will continue even beyond this stage. And once Pyongyang enters the era of a normal relationship with Washington, the safety of the regime and, for that matter, the state will be further strengthened. Nevertheless, if the talks drag on with no significant progress and if normalization is further delayed, the current regime in Pyongyang will be further isolated and its chance for survival will be greatly reduced.[21]

In the long term, the United States can play a meaningful role in securing a peaceful unification on the Korean peninsula. For one thing, because it has no history of invading Korea for territorial gain, America will be relatively free of Korean suspicion as a potential foe of Korean unification. And its role as a balancer and broker in Korean affairs would be least opposed not only by the Koreans themselves but also by the countries surrounding it. Indeed, Washington can and should continue to support Korean unification publicly in order to dispel misperceptions in some quarters of Korean society concerning the United States' intent to engage North Korea. Public statements like that of Acting Assistant Secretary of State Charles Kartman need to be made over and again: "It is not the goal of the United States to see a unified Korean peninsula. It is our goal to support our Korean allies in their efforts first to defend their country and join the United States in a prosperous future, and also if they choose, to unify themselves."[22]

Lastly, the United States can play a leading role in activating the dormant potential for multilateral security dialogue and cooperation in Northeast Asia, most notably by bringing North Korea into international forums. As Kurt Campbell, Deputy Assistant Secretary of Defense for Asia and the Pacific maintained, the United States has multiple goals with respect to the Korean peninsula, including maintaining a strong security alliance with South Korea and "enlarging the scope of the discussion in the region about North Korea. Washington will seek to engage China in a more in-depth manner about what we want to see in the Korean peninsula and what they are prepared to do to support North Korea, coordinating with the ROK and Japan as well."[23]

The Role of China

Since the end of the Cold War, China has been viewed as the main source of threats and arms buildups in East Asia. It has increased its defense spending by over ten percent per annum and continued to modernize its armed forces. It has reinforced outposts on the Spratly Islands, raised tension in the Taiwan Strait by conducting large-scale fire drills, and taken over Hong Kong on July 1, 1997. The growth of China's power in itself is thus perceived as a potential threat to the United States and other regional countries.[24] Indeed, China appears to be the key variable in the uncertain security environment in Northeast Asia. This partly explains why the United States is so sensitive about China's interest in the Korean peninsula.

What, then, would be the role of an increasingly powerful China in maintaining peace and achieving unification in Korea? Probably next to the United States, China can play a significant role in shaping the security environment of the Korean peninsula for the next ten to fifteen years. Especially, China's role in resolving major contingencies in North Korea in cooperation with the United States could be extremely important. At present, Beijing maintains a traditional alliance with Pyongyang, while it continues to improve its chiefly economic ties with Seoul. It is attending the Four-party Talks designed to institute a new peace regime replacing the current armistice regime, as it did at the armistice talks in 1953. Beijing's mediator role between the two Koreas is not very significant at the moment, but it will increase. This unique hedging role of China is worth our special attention as long as North Korea exists as a state. It is fair to say that "China is working to balance its political and economic relations with both North and South Korea in ways that will increase its influence over the shape of any final settlement between the two Koreas."[25]

In the short term, China will apparently prefer the maintenance of the current armistice regime on the Korean peninsula. Because its first priority will continue to be advancing its economic interests, Beijing does not want trouble from its next-door neighbor.[26] It has its own internal problems, which consume a great deal of the time and energy of its leadership. It also has to tackle external problems such as an independence-oriented Taiwan and, more broadly, what the leadership perceives as the containment of China by the United States and its allies. As a corollary of these current internal and external problems, it definitely wants the peaceful coexistence of the two Koreas, i.e., the status quo. China will be more concerned with its confrontational relations with the United States and Japan and will try to check these stronger powers by rejuvenating its relationships with its old allies in Russia and North Korea. In particular, Beijing wants Pyongyang to remain in its sphere of influence, worrying that the improving U.S.-DPRK relationship could end up drawing Pyongyang into Washington's orbit. Beijing's continued fuel supply and its recent decision to provide extra food assistance to the flood-stricken Pyongyang are good examples of its moves in this direction. One negative impact of China's assistance is the diminishing need for North Korea to negotiate seriously with South Korea and consequently Chinese aid contributes to the continuation of the North-South confrontation in Korea.

In the foreseeable future, China will play a low profile, but an important role in maintaining the status quo on the Korean peninsula. It will seek to prevent a sudden collapse of the Kim Jong-il regime, because it would have a devastating impact on China. Beijing presently has an effective defense treaty with Pyongyang, and would respond to major contingencies in North Korea if so asked by its ally in Pyongyang. This will be particularly true as long as the Washington-Beijing relationship remains tense. A major contingency would inevitably invite intervention by the ROK, which constitutionally claims North Korea as part of its territory, and the United States, which would seek an early settlement of the contingency together with the ROK. These interventions without doubt would seriously challenge Beijing. The Chinese leadership will need to make decisions on whether or not, and how, to intervene in Korean affairs if the Pyongyang regime or a pro-Chinese rebel group requests Chinese assistance. China's decisions would in turn have tremendous impact on the actions of South Korea and the United States.

The likelihood of Chinese intervention in North Korean contingencies depends on many factors, and U.S. involvement is certainly one of them. Even though Beijing has long declared nonintervention in the internal affairs of other countries as one of its five principles of peaceful coexistence, it remains to be seen whether it would observe the principle in Korean contingencies. For China, massive numbers of refugees streaming across the border into its territory would be a grave concern and threat. It has already reportedly built some huge camps to accommodate these prospective refugees from North Korea. Also, if American forces, in tandem with South Korea, were to advance deep into the North to respond to a major contingency in North Korea, China may well attempt to counter them for fear of losing a buffer zone. Related to this, the flight of some segments of North Korea's fighting forces into its territory would be another case in which China would have to respond forcefully.

In the long term, however, China will have to decide on how to respond to North and South Korea's drive toward integration and eventual unification. It is true that today many Koreans perceive China as opposed to unification on Seoul's terms. Because China fears what it perceives as American containment, it understandably does not want a near-term unification of Korea under American influence. But as Beijing expands its security dialogue and cooperation not only with Washington but also with Tokyo and Seoul, it will regain confidence in its ability to manage the Korean situation. Moreover, as Washington and Tokyo push for diplomatic normalization with Pyongyang to complete the missing links in a cross-recognition of the two Koreas, Beijing's concern and the future of North Korea will abate. Therefore, as the two Koreas get closer to unification, Beijing will have no choice but to accept it. In other words, it may have to accept a peaceful unified Korea as a better choice for China than the current divided Korea. As long as its territorial integrity is guaranteed, China will not be tempted to oppose Korean unification. The presence and the level of U.S. troops in Korea around the time of Korean unification will turn out to be a matter of debate and negotiation among all the parties concerned.

Once unification is achieved in Korea, China will have to live in harmony with the new neighboring state to the east. Beijing's concern and interest will then be to induce unified Korea to lean toward it or at least to make it friendly. Based on Sino-Korean cultural links and historical affinities, China will exert influence to draw the new Korea into its sphere. As one American analyst rightly observed some years ago, "[The] South Korean perception of China contrasts sharply with popular views of Japan, and may be partially due to cultural links between the two nations and China's relative backwardness."[27] The implication is that, in the distant future as China becomes more advanced and its gap with Korea narrows, the Korean perception will also be likely to change. It will not be as easy as one might imagine to see the two countries allied against the countries around them. Of course, "in a worst-case scenario a unified Korea could catalyze polarization in Northeast Asia: a continental-rimland divide between a Sino-Korean coalition and a renewed U.S.-Japan alliance."[28] In all probability the unified Korea will pursue a freer hand, with strong ties to the United States. Quite naturally, too, the two neighboring countries will have as much disharmony and conflict as they have harmony and cooperation. On the economic side, the two countries will endeavor to utilize their complementary economic structures as much as possible, though amid growing competition.

The Role of Japan

The United States and Japan issued a new joint security declaration in April 1996. Moreover, the two allies adopted new guidelines for defense cooperation designed to deal effectively with contingencies in the region around Japan. These two events reconfirm their security partnership in the post-Cold War era in general and allow for the expansion of Japan's role in and contributions to regional security in particular. With the Russian military threat gone the North Korean threat came into the limelight. Given these changes in the security environment of Northeast Asia, Japan's expanded role is welcomed by the United States, but is severely criticized by

China, which perceives it as part of a U.S. strategy of containment. For North Korea, Japan's expanded role in Korean contingencies is of course irritating. What, if any, would be the role of Japan in the security of the Korean peninsula?

It appears that in the foreseeable future Japan will play a much smaller role than the United States and China in maintaining peace on the Korean peninsula. For one thing, it has not been invited to the Four-party Talks, because it was not a party to the Korean War. Most importantly, as long as there is lingering animosity and a lack of understanding between Korea and Japan, Japan's potential role in bringing peace to Korea will be underrated or even rejected. These stumbling blocks to Japan's positive role will be gradually removed as Japan engages in Korea by normalizing relations with North Korea and by participating in multilateral security forums to deal with Korean and other Northeast Asian security issues. At any rate, Japan, for various historical and political reasons, can presumably make only limited contributions to the establishment of a new peace regime on the Korean peninsula in the near term.

At the root of these negative feelings toward Japan's role might be the Koreans' "psychological sense of *han* (a bitter grudge, full of rancor), with overtones of xenophobic animosity toward those who inflicted harm on Korea."[29] *Han* has been vented against the Japanese for their colonial atrocities. Unless the Japanese sincerely redress the grievances many Koreans have toward them, the Korean-Japanese relationship will likely remain tense and mutual perceptions of threats will be exacerbated. This will be even truer if the two Koreas are unified. In addition, Japan's attitudes and behavior during the process of unification of North and South Korea—e.g., giving the impression that it prefers the current division to unification,—may work to add to Korea's uneasiness about and perception of Japan as a threat. In this sense the following observation is quite to the point: "But precisely to the extent that regional perceptions of Japan are bound by history, any Japanese effort to fill a prospective American security void in Northeast Asia would provoke apprehension, perhaps even alarm, in some of its neighbors, and could have unintended and undesirable consequences."[30]

Besides food assistance and the KEDO project for North Korea, Japan in the future will resume talks with North Korea to discuss normalization of their diplomatic relations. Once normalization is a reality, Tokyo can play a positive role in maintaining peace on the Korean peninsula. For instance, Japan can, if it so decides, easily help North

Korea bolster its backward economy. Even though most Japanese businesses would not be willing to invest heavily in this poor country with few prospects for growth, the Japanese government may provide some financial assistance in the form of subsidized loans. Japan can also use its negotiating cards—such as loans, wartime reparation, and other economic aid and investment—to enhance its influence over North Korea. Along with provision of Official Development Assistance, the Japanese government can induce private capital to move into a new North Korea, and can play an important role in mobilizing international financial institutions such as the Asian Development Bank and the World Bank.

On the defense side, Japan's new National Defense Program Outline (NDPO) of November 1995 and the new guidelines for defense cooperation with the United States will directly or indirectly affect the security of the Korean peninsula. Japan's rear area and other support for American troops in Korean contingencies, for example, would provide the United States with much-needed leverage. Likewise, Japan can and will play a larger role in responding to crises in the Korean peninsula, namely, those that call for the protection and accommodation of massive numbers of refugees in Japan, humanitarian assistance, noncombatant evacuation operations, minesweeping operations, etc. Japan can play an active role in UN, PKO, and UNHCR activities after UN resolutions are passed concerning North Korean contingencies. It can also cooperate with the United States on several issues—for instance putting pressure on Pyongyang to give up the use of military threats and terrorism. Also, it can use the speed and scope of its normalized relations with North Korea in an effort to reduce tension on the peninsula. In sum, in the near future Japan does not seem to be able to play any significant independent role other than that of assisting the United States in playing a predominant role for peace in Korea.

On the external front, Japan's pursuit for a permanent membership in the UN Security Council has been supported by the United States, Germany, and other Western countries; and it will be achieved sometime in the future. Japan's dream of a *seiji taikoku,* or big political power, will thus be realized, and Japan will play a role commensurate with its economic power. In its competition with China over the Korean peninsula, Japan may make a very careful move toward various pending issues with the two Koreas, including potential disputes over maritime sovereignty, the newly declared Exclusive Economic Zone, and military modernization programs.

In the longer term, however, Japan can and will play a bigger role in bringing about a unified Korea. At present, most Japanese are not as concerned with Korean unification and Japan's role in it as many Koreans perceive. But in the future, when the two Koreas are much closer to unification, Japan will likely see more benefits than losses from Korean unification. A unified Korea, for example, can remain a strong buffer zone between Japan and China, and can lessen political friction among the three Asian countries. Furthermore, it would be easier, as one analyst suggests, for Japan to resolve the issue of Korean claims for damage done during the Japanese colonial rule in Korea.[31]

The Role of Russia

It may be fair to say that for a very long period of time Russia will play, relative to the other three big powers, the role of a lesser, peripheral actor with regard to Korean security. For good reason, Russia will be least able to exert any assertive influence over the course of the future Korea. Not only will it have to wrestle with many political and economic problems domestically, but it will also be least influenced by developments on the Korean peninsula. Because it has nothing much to fear from North Korean contingencies and Korean unification, its concern and interest in Korean security is not as great as that of China or Japan. Geographical distance, the relatively short history of contacts with the two Koreas, and different levels of economic development all account for Russia's disadvantages in engaging in Korean affairs. Russia nevertheless can and will play a checks-and-balances role with regard to developments on the peninsula if its national interest is severely threatened. In other words, Russia can and will play some active role, in the sense that it can impede any major developments on the Korean peninsula that would endanger Russian interests.

In the near future, Moscow will continue to improve its relations with Seoul despite its discontent with the way the ROK government has treated it, including the lower-than-expected level of economic exchange, exclusion from the Four-party Talks proposal, and a lack of interest in large acquisitions of Russian weapons and equipment. If the collapse of the current North Korean regime becomes more likely, Russia will remain cool to the Pyongyang regime. Even in the case of major contingencies in North Korea, Russia is least likely to intervene. Moscow has already lost much of its influence over Pyongyang because of weakened relations with its old ally; and although Russia seeks to restore relations, it does not seem to expect much from the failing Pyongyang regime. On Pyongyang's part, the sense of being discarded by Moscow remains strong. This partly explains why Pyongyang has actively pursued normalizing relations with Washington and, to a lesser degree, Tokyo.

In retrospect, starting from the end of 1993, Russia's Korea policy has changed from a Seoul-centered diplomacy to the restoration of its normal relations with Pyongyang. So far this has not been very successful. But as Russia's external policy becomes more traditional, and especially so toward the Korean peninsula, South Korea fears that Moscow will try to reuse its North Korea cards. The abrogation of a treaty of friendly cooperation and mutual assistance in 1996, for example, restrains Pyongyang's maneuverability. By abrogating the treaty, Russia can keep itself from being involved militarily in major contingencies on the Korean peninsula. It can also improve its image and remove obstacles to expanded relations with South Korea. Finally, it can lower its political, military, and psychological burden and turn its relationship with North Korea into a normal relationship between neighbors. The conclusion of a new treaty would provide another occasion to normalize relations between the two countries.

There seems nothing much for Russia to do other than joining UN Security Council resolutions in response to major North Korean contingencies. However, it will continue to play an active role in advancing multilateral security dialogues and cooperation in Northeast Asia, because these are the best mechanisms by which Russia can compensate for its weakest position vis-à-vis the Korean peninsula and earn the most profits for the least investment. Moscow will certainly continue this very profitable enterprise in the future. It will seek to take advantage of the various proposals of collective security arrangements and many other multilateral initiatives.[32] In addition, it is expected that Russia, though slightly different from China in its approach, can actively participate in multilateral maritime cooperation inspired by law-of-the-sea issues and cooperation on minor rescue missions.[33] To be sure, Russia has good reason to reemphasize its long-held interests in this region and thus to reexamine its previous multilateral proposals. The economic development of Siberia, the Maritime Provinces, and Russian Asia in general is the precondition for any effective Russian role in Asia's economy and politics. In fact, Russia has continued to stress its ties to Japan, and the broader vision of a cooperative multilateralism in Northeast Asia that includes the two Koreas.[34]

With regard to creating a new peace regime in Korea, Russia is willing to participate in six-country talks [i.e., Four-party Talks plus

Russia and Japan], where it can check and balance the increasing influence of the United States and China over Korea. It can at least play a guarantor role for the two Koreas' search for a permanent peace, and will quite likely become involved in various other multilateral forums dealing with Korean issues. Finally, as the two Koreas approach unification and as Russia recovers from decades of political instability and economic slump, Moscow can and will enhance its "constructive" influence on Korea.

RELATIONS AMONG THE MAJOR POWERS
The Impact of U.S.-China Rivalry

Many keen observers of East Asian affairs view the future relationship between the United States and China as one of the most important factors in regional security. This is predicated upon several long-term prospects that include the maintenance of a close U.S.-Japan relationship, increasing threats of Chinese regional hegemony,[35] the end of the Russian threat, and the perception of a reduced U.S. role in the Asia-Pacific region. Most of these givens will be subject to change as the East Asian strategic equilibrium evolves.[36] Nevertheless, the rivalry and cooperation between the United States and China would certainly create new challenges and threat perceptions as well as opportunities. Equally plausible would be a cooperative security environment through continuous talks and arbitration, and increased transparency among the regional powers.

The China threat debate had been in full swing until recently when Washington actively engaged itself in a security dialogue with Beijing. Obviously, China has shown growing concern and even worry about what it perceives as U.S. containment, which it believes entered its final stage with the linkage between Japan and a country in the southern flank, namely Australia. These two countries are viewed as the "two claws of a crab" that are poised against China. Yet it appears that the debate in the United States has begun to lose its fervor. The containment versus engagement debate seems partly flagging in favor of the latter. Still, will the China threat decline in the years to come? Whatever the answer, the U.S.-China relationship will have an undeniably significant impact on the security environment of Northeast Asia, and, if less visible at present, on the Korean peninsula.

What seems promising, however, is the start of a security dialogue and cooperation between the United States and China. While pushing for a "constructive engagement," Washington demands that China become a responsible member of the world community. As Robert

Sutter rightly indicates, multilateral engagement with China would presumably have the objective of demonstrating to the Chinese leadership that their concerns about the intentions of others have been exaggerated and that China has more to gain from a continued cooperative approach toward the region.[37] If this trend continues, American knowledge, and understanding of China will grow, and the American perception of a Chinese threat will abate with time. In fact, many China analysts concur that the China threat has been exaggerated and that it would take China some twenty to thirty years to catch up with today's American military capabilities. If things work together in this way, a non-hostile China with a huge economy will emerge. After another fifteen years of sustained economic growth, and a sweeping military reform, China will probably play a stabilizing role in making peace and furthering unification in Korea rather than the opposite.

In the near term, because of the lingering American perception of a Chinese threat and the Chinese perception of American containment, the two giants will probably be at odds over many Korean issues, especially at the Four-party Talks. China will not want a sudden collapse of the Kim Jong-il regime and extensive American intervention in such contingencies. Beijing might use the issue of the U.S. military presence in Korea as a negotiating card. The United States, for its part, will seek to explain the rationale for continued forward deployment of its forces in Korea and to reach a common understanding on how to deal with major contingencies in North Korea. In particular, controlling North Korea's biochemical weapons in the event of major contingencies will be given a high priority in negotiations between Washington and Beijing. In any event, U.S.-China cooperation over the settlement of disputes in the Korean peninsula will be increasingly important and inevitable.

In the longer term, as the two Koreas continue to progress toward integration and unification, the rivalry between Washington and Beijing over drawing Korea into their respective spheres of influence will be intensified. This will presumably pressure the two Koreas, or the unified Korea, to review their alliance relationships, and decide on a future course. In the process there may be some compromise between the two powers, and this again will impact Korea's security environment and security strategy at the time.

ROK-U.S.-Japan Trilateral Security Cooperation

During the Cold War the U.S. successfully maintained a close security alliance with Japan and the ROK to deter any military conflict in East Asia. Alliance with the two countries has been a success story for both. Japan has become the world's second leading economic power, and the ROK achieved much of its economic growth since the alliance. In the post-Cold War period, the U.S. has actively engaged in regional security, strengthening its bilateral and multilateral security cooperation with most countries in the region. At present, the major issue facing the ROK, United States, and Japan is undoubtedly the likelihood of major contingencies in North Korea. These events, in whatever form, would greatly impact all the neighboring countries. How to prevent and, if prevention fails, how to settle these crises most effectively are the dominant concern for all the regional actors.

Consequently, Washington and Seoul, in cooperation with Tokyo, have been actively engaged in making plans for any possible major contingency in North Korea. The new guidelines for U.S.-Japan defense cooperation are designed, among other things, to deal with these contingencies. If these guidelines become highly visible, it may well have some negative impact on China's potential role in North Korean contingencies. In this context, Washington has presumably sought Beijing's cooperation on the matter, and the effort will continue throughout the Four-party Talks. But for the time being, because of the tense relationship between Washington and Beijing, only the three countries (ROK, U.S., Japan) will, in one way or another, cooperate in the contingency planning.

U.S. leadership and the role Washington will undertake are extremely important in implementing contingency plans. With forward-deployment and long-distance power projection capability, the United States can and will play an important role as a stabilizer and balancer. And as Washington improves its bilateral relations with Pyongyang, its role will even be expanded. Indeed, as Ralph Cossa rightly points out, the United States remains a major player economically and continues to provide a "political and economic model that, with minor modifications to fit Asian culture, continues to be attractive."[38]

In the longer term, as the North Korean crisis is managed and the two Koreas enter the phase of accommodation and integration, the three countries will work together to shape an environment favorable to Korean unification. In parallel, the trilateral security participants (Republic of Korea, the U.S., and Japan) will also consider preparations for expanded multilateral cooperation involving China, Russia, and North Korea. In so doing, primary emphasis will be placed on improving U.S. relations with China, which will have a tremendous, if indirect, impact on Korean unification. It is, therefore, imperative not only that

the United States and China expand their security dialogue and cooperation, but also that the U.S., Japan, and the ROK expand the horizon
of their cooperation to engage China, Russia, and North Korea.

Multilateral Security Cooperation

Multilateral security forums are burgeoning in number in today's
Asia-Pacific region. They include APEC, ASEAN-PMC, ARF,
NAFTA, East Asian Economic Cooperation (EAEC), the U.S.-pro-
posed NEACD (Northeast Asia Cooperation Dialogue), the ROK-pro-
posed NEASD (North East Asian Security Dialogue), the Council for
Security Cooperation in the Asia Pacific (CSCAP), and most recently,
the Japan-proposed Forum for Defense Authorities in the Asia Pacific
region.[39] Many of these forums can serve as venues for discussing
and settling many security issues related to the Korean peninsula. South
Korea has been very cooperative in these multilateral efforts and instrumental in the creation of several multilateral mechanisms, one of its
contributions to the making of the New World Order.[40] For instance, in
May 1993 the ROK government made a proposal for a mini-CSCE for
Northeast Asia, in tandem with an expanded ASEAN-PMC security
dialogue. Indeed, the ROK is ready to utilize multilateral security forums in its effort to maintain peace and achieve unification.

The Korean question, which at the moment is the most urgent
question with wide-ranging impact on the security of Northeast Asia,
will be a convenient item on the agenda for these multilateral efforts.
The most immediate concern at any multilateral forum dealing with the
Korean question would be provisions of various kinds of assistance to
famine-stricken North Korea. At the Four-party Talks, for example,
this issue will be heavily discussed, even though the main purpose of
the talks is to secure a new peace regime on the Korean peninsula.

Another topic for multilateral security forums would be how to
deal with major contingencies in North Korea. Later, by the time
the two Koreas approach unification, multilateral security cooperation will be more securely in place. Korean unification and its implications will be widely discussed at these forums. The internationalization of the issue of Korean unification will have more of a
positive than a negative impact on the unification process.

Security Environment: Threats and Dangers Around Year 2010

Many believe that differing rates of economic growth among the
strong powers in Northeast Asia may cause growing tensions and threat
perceptions. Around the year 2000, Korea will still be a small power

relative to the countries around it. With its continued economic growth, China will likely join the economic status of an advanced country. Japan, for all its domestic political problems, will maintain economic power and a technological edge. Russia will begin to regain strength. The United States is likely to keep its edge as the only superpower for the next several years in the post Cold-War era and will quite likely maintain its military presence at a reduced level while still wielding powerful influence on regional security. The threat environment envisioned in Northeast Asia for this period of time—the onset of the twenty-first century—will probably be characterized by such factors as conflicts between economic blocs, conflicts over strategically important sea lines of communication, territorial disputes over islands and the continental shelf, accidents at sea, and maritime pollution.[41]

First, despite many equally persuasive arguments to the contrary, the United States will continue to maintain its leadership and play an indispensable role as a balancer of power, stabilizer, and honest broker in this region.[42] Whether or not the United States can play these roles, however, will depend heavily on domestic pressure at the time. Some Americans have predicted that negative attitudes toward the envisioned regional role for the United States with a troop presence in Korea will make it politically hard to implement.[43] And changes in U.S policy may alter America's ability to implement its global security policy.

Second, China certainly has its own strengths and weaknesses. There seems to be no royal road to economic, political, technological, and military development for any country, and thus China will find obstacles to its progress at least around the turn of the century.[44] Even if advanced in terms of economic outputs, China will remain relatively inward-looking with its own domestic problems. Its armed forces will undergo forced modernization, yet its military power will not go unchecked, though a higher level of military transparency will be required. Thus, China may play a necessary, if limited, mediating role in securing stability on the Korean peninsula.

Some of the threats China might pose to other countries around the time of Korean unification include a strong Chinese navy with blue-water capability, sea pollution caused by many industrial cities along the coast of the Yellow Sea, territorial claims to certain islands, and border clashes on the mainland. One potential area of conflict is Manchuria, where many ethnic Koreans have lived for generations. In fact, the Chinese are concerned about the spillover of these ethnic Koreans' claim to the area because China comprises a multitude of ethnic minorities.[45]

Third, Japan will continue to expand its security role in the years to come. As can be seen in the new joint security declaration with the United States in April 1996, Japan has chosen to expand its global partnership with the U.S. into East Asia. It will certainly hope to play many additional low-profile roles, mindful of negative reactions from neighboring countries. While so doing, Japan is likely to expand security cooperation with these countries to alleviate their concerns and worries. There will be growing concern among many Koreans about Tokyo's continuous claim to Tokto islet and its perceived scheme to dominate East Asia.[46] On the other hand, many Japanese have recently expressed increasing concern about the Korean perception of the Japanese threat.[47]

Fourth, Russia will be more forthcoming in pushing for its interests in the region. Once domestic politics and the economy are on the right track, the Russians will quite likely exert their influence in regional affairs, including security issues on the Korean peninsula. In particular, they will become more active in multilateral security dialogue and cooperation in Northeast Asia.

Finally, unified Korea around the year 2010 and thereafter will likely face other sources of threats and conflicts. Competition and cooperation between the United States and China would certainly create new challenges and threat perceptions as well as opportunities. There seem to be countless newly emerging threats in this highly dynamic part of the world. On the other hand, it is often equally plausible that a cooperative security environment through continuous talks and arbitration, and increased transparency among the regional powers could emerge.

The current crisis of the North Korean regime undoubtedly poses threats to ROK security, but, if properly managed, it can also be a great opportunity for ROK defense policy planning. Put differently, the ROK can turn the current challenges into opportunities if it develops a new defense vision and defense concept, and puts them into practice accordingly. Emphasis should be placed on developing South Korea's self-sufficient defense and on dealing with newly emerging missions, while maintaining the ROK-U.S. alliance and engaging in multilateral security arrangements.

As for the defense policy of a unified Korea, the ROK can learn from U.S. experiences in formulating its new defense policy for the next century. As the United States reviewed its military strategy after the Gulf War, the ROK needs to review its own after North Korea's threat significantly declines. Even if North Korea's threat declines, however, uncertainty in the security environment may increase. Therefore, the ROK will need to design a defense strategy, though in an atmosphere of uncertainty, that moves away from threat-based planning to mission-based planning.[48] As the nature of threats and conflicts change, the ROK armed forces will also need to consider many missions requiring Operations Other Than War (OOTW).[49] In addition, more concerted efforts will be required to upgrade navy and air force equipment, increase capability for dealing with OOTW, extend military cooperation with many other non-Northeast Asian countries, exercise preventive and coercive diplomacy over disputed territories, and maintain UN peacekeeping and enforcement activities.

In the twenty-first century, achieving an advanced defense will require completing many tasks. These include effective use of the defense budget, standardization in logistics and defense industry, development of dual-use technology, and a higher level of military welfare. ROK defense policy after the year 2010 needs to place more emphasis on these traditionally neglected issues. As General Yong-Ok Park, the current Assistant Minister of National Defense for Policy concludes, unified Korea "should continuously engage in combating malpractice within itself and in creating a credible force that meets the requirements of future warfare and the defense of a unified Korea. Introduction of civilian management methods and foreign defense systems should be designed to structure a defense management system that guarantees a reliable military force with limited resources. The military should always assist national development projects and work together with society as one."[50]

CONCLUSION

Divided Korea, and later unified Korea, will continue to be a security pivot in Northeast Asia. In the foreseeable future, the possibility of the collapse of the current North Korean regime and the impact of such contingencies will dominate the concerns of all the neighboring countries, as well as the ROK. If the Kim Jong-il regime survives this crisis, it will go through various openings and reforms. In this process of integration and unification, the two Koreas will play the most decisive roles, though neighboring countries will play significant roles as well. The United States in particular will be an important actor which also has much at stake in the region.

Regarding the threat from the North, even if it declines, ROK defense planners should consider the likelihood of an impending collapse of the Pyongyang regime. They should also consider the likelihood that the two Koreas will enter an interim phase of accommodation and integration. In other words, a soft-landing for North Korea is better than its sudden collapse for the ROK's planning purposes. ROK defense policy should also be flexible and adaptive enough to accommodate types of threats other than conventional warfare and other contingencies in North Korea.

In the longer term, a growing interdependence between nations makes multilateral dialogues and cooperation inevitable. With such increasingly visible changes in the security environment in Northeast Asia, there will be an increasing demand for multilateral security dialogue and cooperation among the regional countries. In particular, the United States, Japan, and the ROK—as well as China, Russia, and even North Korea—can play extremely important roles in securing a new peace regime and an eventual unification on the Korean peninsula.

For the future Korea, the American connection is the best alternative for securing its mid- to long-term security and independence, and for resisting encroachment by neighboring powers. Surveying the possibilities for the future, as one American analyst put it, "the case for a continuing American security partnership with Korea would seem to be strong—even if the North Korean threat is removed and a free and peaceful reunification is consummated."[51]

Finally, the following remark should serve as the guide for the unified Korea's external policy: "If there are lessons to be drawn from these examples, they would include these: do not exaggerate a country's potential threat; do not imagine a threat just because it is ideologically compelling to do so; do consider the question of timing when responding to a real threat; do seek multilateral, regional solutions to a bilateral crisis. I do believe these lessons are relevant today."[52]

Chapter Three
Japan

Japan has the world's second largest economy, with a GDP $2.5 trillion greater than that of the third-ranking German economy; it is also the pillar of the U.S. alliance system in Asia. Korean unification could, however, upset the regional equilibrium. An end to the Korean conflict could lead, in rapid succession, to the dismantlement of the U.S. military presence in East Asia and the rise of tensions between Japan and its mainland neighbors. As a result, Japan's peace and prosperity would be at greater risk than at any time since 1945. In ten years Northeast Asia could become unstable, with its economy damaged by a loss of confidence in the continued peace and prosperity of the region.

Korean unification, or any peaceful end to the Korean conflict (such as a credible peace treaty between South and North Korea), could lead to the contingencies outlined below. Not all these events are mutually exclusive, but neither are they all likely to materialize. Nevertheless, the combination of even a few of these developments could undermine Japan's security.

American Withdrawal from Northeast Asia

As long as a North Korean menace exists, the American military deployment in Northeast Asia will probably enjoy continued support from the Congress and Executive Branch. Once Korea is united, however, the American military presence in Northeast Asia might well end, or be drastically reduced. Should Korean unification lead to the departure of U.S. forces from the region, it would be catastrophic for Japan because the U.S. connection is the key to its security. The U.S. military presence, especially the ground forces, provides three functions, all of which are crucial for Japan.

First, the American military maintains a stable balance of power in Northeast Asia which is favorable to Japan. As the table on the following page indicates, Japan alone is not particularly strong militarily compared with its neighbors:

Military Power in Northeast Asia - 1996[1]

	A.	B.	C.	D.	E.
U.S.	253	1484	10,497	Yes	Yes
Japan	45-62	235	1,130	No	No
China	8-32(?)	2935	8,250	No	Yes
Taiwan	14	376	630+	No	No
ROK	16	660	2,050	No	No
DPRK	2-5(?)	1054	3,400	No	(?)
Russia	48	1270	16,800	(?)	Yes

A. Defense budget 1996 ($ billion).
B. Personnel (in thousands).
C. Tanks.
D. Strategic air-sea lift capability.
E. Weapons of mass destruction.

These figures do not reflect the qualitative differences between Japan's first-world military and the forces of less developed countries. Nevertheless, they indicate that, without the U.S. alliance, Japan's military resources are not capable of maintaining a clear-cut regional superiority.

Second, the visible presence of U.S. forces, in the form of bases and soldiers, is a tangible reminder of the American commitment to the U.S.-Japan alliance. Even if the two countries remained closely allied after Korean unification, the departure of American forces would be interpreted as a de facto termination, or at least a severe downgrading, of the alliance. Moreover, in a military or diplomatic emergency, the United States would find it more difficult and costly to redeploy to the region once its infrastructure there had been dismantled.

Third, the U.S. military presence reassures Japan's neighbors. For various reasons, many Asian nations, especially China and Korea, are wary of Japanese power. American servicemen in Asia, including 47,000 in Japan, reassure Asians that Japan will not use its economic supremacy to dominate Asia politically and militarily. Consequently, the United States makes it possible for Japanese businesses to trade and invest in Asia without rousing undue fears of "Japanese imperialism." These fears are based on Japan's past rather than on its contemporary reality, but they are firmly held, extremely potent, and potentially harmful to Japan's interests in Asia.

In Korea, some nationalists deplore the presence of foreign soldiers in their country. To these Koreans, U.S. troops (whose Seoul quarters housed Japanese soldiers before 1945) symbolize national humiliation. The United States planned Korea's division in 1945, and in 1953 acquiesced to the accord which has come to perpetuate it. In both cases America imposed the settlement on Koreans (the ROK opposed the armistice, and Koreans were excluded from the 1945 Soviet-American agreement). Some Koreans also reproach the United States for its strong ties to Japan, including its acquiescence in Japan's occupation of Korea in the early twentieth century, and its lenient treatment of Japan during the Occupation (many Koreans favored hanging the emperor as a prelude to a Carthaginian peace). Some, too, blame the Americans for the Kwangju incident in 1980 because they believe that the U.S. Army commander authorized the use of ROK troops in the city.

The American military presence also impedes Korean autonomy. A united Korea might want to act as a balancing force among China, Russia, Japan, and the United States; American troops in Korea, however, would be incompatible with a policy of equidistance among the great powers. Thus, nationalism and a desire for more freedom of action might lead to a successful political campaign to rid the country of foreign (i.e., U.S.) troops after unification. This is unlikely because most Korean policymakers realize that a strong U.S.-Korean military relationship is the best policy to safeguard Korean security and independence, but nevertheless possible because the impact of nationalism is difficult to predict. In addition, Korea has a high population density, and American soldiers occupy land Koreans think could be put to better use. (For example, in Seoul, the U.S. army is still settled in a large compound in the heart of this crowded metropolis). Because South Koreans are far richer than thirty years ago, (not withstanding the recent problems) they no longer see the Americans as an important source of foreign exchange which compensates for the social cost of their presence on Korean soil.

In Japan, too, movements could arise that favor the closing American bases. Part of the rationale for the existence of American forces in Japan is their role in defending Korea, which is Japan's first line of defense. Unification, consequently, will make justifying that deployment much more difficult.

Like South Korea, Japan also lacks the wide open spaces of the United States which allow American servicemen to train effectively without disturbing too many residents. The land requirements, noise, and social disturbances brought about by the presence of GIs accordingly create opposition to them. Further, even more than South Korea,

Japan is so rich that a few tens of thousands of servicemen are economically insignificant to the nation, especially since Japanese taxpayers subsidize them. Opponents of the U.S. military presence, then, can also mobilize the permanent displeasure of many Japanese over the environmental and human costs of the American bases.

The situation in Okinawa makes these issues particularly salient. U.S. ground forces in Japan are concentrated on Okinawa, south of the home islands. The stationing of 28,000 U.S. service personnel (21,000 of them marines) breeds resentment. Political and grass-root groups have arisen that want to free their island of the marines. The 1996 agreement to return some land to Okinawans has stabilized the situation, but it is unclear for how long. In fact, no Japanese communities would welcome U.S. servicemen, should the latter have to relocate, without the U.S. and Japanese governments undertaking an effective and well-orchestrated public relations campaign. The removal of U.S. forces from Okinawa could therefore mark the end of the U.S. ground presence in Japan.

The end of the Korean conflict could, in addition, rekindle the energy of Japanese pacifists. Thus, for fundamentalist pacifists, peace in Korea will provide a new impulse to close U.S. bases in Japan.

Yet another source of opposition to the U.S. military deployment in Asia can be found in the United States itself. As long as there is a risk of war in Korea, the views of these opponents of deployment are unlikely to prevail. Not even President Carter could overcome established opinion on the matter. He had to relent on his plan to bring American soldiers home from Korea. Once Korea is unified, this state of affairs will change.

Isolationist ideologues will probably not cause the change in policy. Rabid isolationism, xenophobic and protectionist, is likely to remain a minority position in America.[2] If there is an American withdrawal from Asia at all, it will result from the decisions of mainstream politicians of both parties. These politicians are likely to explain that, with North Korea eliminated and Russia weak and democratic, they see no reason to base forces in the western Pacific, where their only purpose will be to provoke China. Budget cutters will exploit the occasion to slash Pentagon spending. While keeping U.S. forces in Japan is cheaper than keeping them in the U.S. because of host nation support, disbanding them altogether would be even less costly. Based on a similar reasoning, the United States undertook a military and diplomatic withdrawal from Europe after the collapse of the Soviet Union (which contributed to aggravating the consequences of the breakup of Yugoslavia).

As a result of converging pressures from Korea, Japan, and the United States, then, American forces might leave Northeast Asia following Korea's unification. The reasons for this withdrawal would not matter much; what will be significant is that for the first time since 1945 there would be no American ground presence in the region.

KOREAN STRATEGIC AUTONOMY AND MILITARY POTENTIAL

The need for American support in defending against the North prevents the ROK from implementing a national security policy which deviates too much from American desires. (The South is richer than the North and could forego American protection, but the risks of war and the cost of deterrence would rise dramatically). Yet after unification the ROK's policies will no longer need to dovetail with those of the United States Because of the Korean citizenry's animosity toward Japan, there are Japanese who fear that Korea's new government might become unfriendly toward the country.

After unification, the ROK forces will be freed from the need to concentrate on the Northern threat. Simultaneously, South Korea will inherit from North Korea a large pool of trained soldiers and reservists in addition to the North's nuclear program (which, even if it was "frozen" by the Framework Agreement, must still have some potential.) The unified country will also have the North's supply of crude, but potentially lethal, ballistic missiles.

An independent and united Korea is disturbing to Japan because a lack of Japanese understanding of Korea combined with the reality of the prevalence of anti-Japanese feelings in Korea and makes some Japanese fear Sino-Korean cooperation which would isolate Japan. In order to make sense of Japan's fears one must briefly review the historical background of Korean-Japanese ties.

Korea and Japan have much in common. Their cultures bear the imprint of Chinese civilization, which reached Japan through Korea. Some historians believe that the ancestors of the Japanese, and of the Imperial Family, migrated from Korea in ancient times. In the twentieth century Japan colonized Korea, and its influence on Korea is visible today. The late president Park Chung-Hee launched a forced march to industrial modernization in the 1960s which owed much to the nineteenth-century Japanese example.

Proximity, however, has not bred friendship. Koreans remember the Japanese invasions of the late sixteenth century. More importantly, the occupation and colonization of Korea (1905-45) fostered deep hostility. Most ex-colonies enjoy a love-hate relationship with their former suzerain. In the Korean case, however, there is little or no love though there is grudging respect. Since independence, Korean governments (North and South) have striven to erase traces of Japan's rule.

There are several reasons for Korea's dislike of Japan. First among these is the repression and psychological humiliations Koreans experienced during the colonial era. Japanese authorities executed independence activists and relegated the Korean language to a subordinate position. They also transformed the Royal Palace in Seoul into a zoo, altered place names, and in the last years of the colonial regime, forced Koreans to adopt Japanese personal names. They also ordered Koreans to bow to Japanese shinto idols (a particularly repugnant gesture for Korean Christians). Finally, during World War II, the Japanese authorities kidnapped Korean women whom they used as sex slaves for Japanese soldiers (the "comfort women").

Koreans are additionally disturbed by the lack of Japanese contrition. Some look upon Imperial Japan as Asia's Nazi Germany, and believe that postwar Japan should have imitated (West) Germany in acknowledging its past. Koreans find it appalling that, on issues such as the comfort women, Japan's apologies have been so late in coming and confined to understated paraphrases.

One illustration of the Japanese attitude which Koreans (and Chinese) resent is the planned World War II museum in Tokyo. The construction of this $120 million government-financed project started in 1996. It "will focus solely on the suffering of Japanese families and soldiers," and the conservative War Bereaved Families Association will run it.[3] Because the Japanese public is ill-informed about the war in Asia, many Japanese fail to understand how loathsome such memorials are to those who see themselves as victims of Japanese militarism.

Today, South Korea is a "quasi-ally"[4] of Japan. Japan and the ROK are not formally allied, but both are American allies who were on the same side during the Cold War. They have significant trade ties. South Korea relied heavily on Japanese imports to develop its economy, and its industrial and economic policies show the mark of Japanese influence. Moreover, South Korean troops on the DMZ defend Japan as well as their own country. But South Korea is a nation with which Japan does not feel at ease. Political relations are limited, and military connections are only emerging slowly. Some Koreans still consider Japan a potential foe.

Korea's economy is much smaller than Japan's. Yet there are Japanese who fear the military imbalance between the two states because a united Korea will, in some areas of military strength, be more powerful, as the following table shows:

Armed Forces[5] :	Servicemen Active/Reserves	WMDs*	Ball. Missiles
Japan	235/48	No	No
S. + N. Korea	1,714/9,200	Possible	Yes

* Weapons of mass destruction

Some Japanese think that united Korea will merge the South's relatively modern arsenal with some of North Korea's large armed forces and nuclear program. Already a few South Koreans believe that rather than demobilize the North's one million soldiers, the newly unified ROK should retain at least some of them, equipping them with modern weapons and thus creating a large modern army.[6] These are very much minority views, ungrounded in reality; but they have the capacity to generate unease in Japan. Some Japanese already think that a number of South Korea's weapons acquisitions, such as submarines and maritime patrol aircraft, indicate that Korea sees Japan as a rival.

The uproar in South Korea over Tokto (Takeshima in Japanese and Liancourt Rocks on Western maps) illustrates how easily Korean feelings against Japan can be inflamed. Tokto, an islet between Japan and Korea, is claimed by both nations but under the sovereignty of South Korea. Japanese claims to fishing rights around Tokto triggered angry anti-Japanese demonstrations in Korea. Under a united Korea, more incidents like Tokto would be a greater problem for Japan. Currently, the division of the peninsula and the U.S. military presence severely limits South Korea's ability to turn nationalist outrage into more than angry words. Once Korea is unified, and especially in the absence of U.S. presence, Tokto or other disputes could degenerate into more acute disputes.

A stronger and autonomous Korea would not necessarily act on its anti-Japanese instincts. United Korea will face many challenges, and its government is likely to conclude that it still needs United States protection and that it must therefore have good relations with Japan, America's major ally in Asia. Moreover, Japan and Korea do not share a land border, and united Korea is unlikely to have sufficient air and naval power to threaten Japan, especially as long as Japan is allied to the United States. Nevertheless, unification will present a potential challenge to Japan. For the first time in a century it will face a unified and independent Korea.

CHINA AND KOREAN UNIFICATION

The PRC wants peace in the region so that outsiders will engage in business with it. At least until recently, Beijing has discreetly given its blessing to the U.S. military presence in Korea because American forces deter the North from starting a war. Once the threat of war is gone, however, China may decide that it is only natural for Korea to (re)enter the sphere of Chinese influence. Beijing may seek to drive Korea away from its close political and military ties with the United States and business connections with America and Japan. Already China seems to be far less happy with the U.S. military presence in Asia than it was a few years ago. Korean unification will accentuate that trend and China will become even more inclined to seek an end to the U.S. role as an Asian power.

Until 1945, the Japanese assumed that their country's welfare required Japanese influence, if not hegemony in China.[7] An independent China or one controlled by Western nations was deemed a mortal threat. Moreover, China absorbed about 25 percent of Japanese exports in the 1920s, and the "China market was thought to have almost boundless potentialities.[8] In the 1930s China received 80 percent of all Japanese foreign investment.[9] The China question made and broke political coalitions in Tokyo.[10] In addition, China provided a base for the Japanese army to escape civilian control.[11]

After 1945, both the possibility of, and the need for, dominion on the mainland evaporated. China passed into unfriendly hands in 1949, but U.S. protection mitigated the impact on Japanese security. New patterns realigned Japan's foreign economic relations, making China a minor factor in Japan's trade and investment.

Japan did negotiate trade memoranda with the People's Republic. These satisfied businesses wished to sell to China, but were sufficiently low-key to avoid American wrath.[12] After the United States normalized relations with the PRC, Japan established formal diplomatic ties, and assisted China's economic development.

During the era of Sino-Soviet hostility, Japan was an important counterweight to Soviet power for China because it provided a base for the U.S. military and contributed to China's economic development. Sino-Japanese relations, however, did not entail military links, and ties remained confined to the economic sphere.

In past decades, Japan has been very useful to China. It has been an important market for Chinese goods, and lavished development assistance on the PRC. Between 1979 and 1995, the Japanese government provided the PRC with ¥1,610 billion ($14bn) in loans, representing 40 percent of total foreign government loans.[13] Japanese investment is essential for China's economic strategy—which is to offer foreigners the opportunity to manufacture exports with Chinese labor and to gain access to Chinese consumers. Japan is the third largest foreign investor in China, after Hong Kong and Taiwan (both of whom are only partly "foreign" to China).[14] Without Japanese commerce, China's economic performance in the past two decades would have been considerably less impressive.

Nevertheless, China remains wary of Japan. In fact, the greater Japan's role in Chinese economic life, the more likely Beijing will be troubled. Japan has lost its usefulness as an objective ally against the Soviet threat,[15] and the Soviet collapse increased its relative weight in East Asia. Nevertheless, because Japan has not altered its military and diplomatic course, Chinese policy toward Japan has not changed dramatically. China's government needs Japan's economic contribution and, as long as the latter stays the course, Beijing has no reason to modify its Japan policy.

A Chinese attempt to bring Korea under its influence after unification would require Japan to revisit its China policy. As of now, there are competing views of China in Japan. The first sees that country as a military threat, the second as a competing consumer of energy and raw materials, the third as a troubled neighbor who should be helped. These views can be briefly described as follows.

China as a Military Threat. Recent Chinese actions have soured the Japanese view of China—e.g., its naval activities in the South China Sea and the Taiwan Straits, nuclear tests (until very recently), and revived claims to the Japanese Senkaku islands (Diaoyu). The Japanese are also concerned about mineral rights in the East China Sea and the security of the Sea Lanes of Communications (SLOCs), which the development of a PLA power projection capability might endanger.[16] China's aggressive posturing and abusive language is particularly shocking to Japan because its behavior on the international stage is so restrained and devoid of the mildest threats of coercion.

As of yet, there is no alarm in Japan about China. China's military does not present a danger to Japan, and the U.S. presence remains formidable. There are, however, concerns about China's future military course, especially if the country's economy continues to grow.

Japanese fear China, though it is still weak, is growing stronger, and may well seek regional supremacy.

China as a Competitor for Resources. A second Japanese view of China is that rising Chinese consumption of food and oil will spur rivalry between the two countries for resources.[17] While a scholar like Kent Calder of Princeton University sees competition for energy as a source of instability in Asia,[18] this "threat" is unlikely to materialize. Predictions of impending shortages of raw materials have always proved groundless. For example, the gloomy scenarios of the Club of Rome and the Carter Administration's *Global 2000* report were wrong, as Herman Kahn's prescient writings foresaw.[19] Market forces motivate further exploration for resources, and foster new technologies. Moreover, oil and food markets are global. Whether extra demand originates from China or Brazil does not impact Japan any more than it does Uruguay and vice versa.

It is possible, however, that the perception of dwindling resources might worsen tensions in the region. But, while perceived energy or food shortages might contribute to rising tensions, they will not be their primary cause.

China as a Country in Need of Help. Many Japanese worry more about China's weaknesses than about its strengths.[20] They fear that China could break up or enter one of the periods of chaos which have marred its history. They recognize that China is particularly vulnerable now. The transition from Maoism has opened the door to upheavals. The central government's authority is dwindling, yet no alternative system exists to maintain order. Besides political issues, environmental degradation could also destabilize the country. For example, ecological mismanagement of water resources could make it difficult for China to feed itself. Given such a scenario, China's regime could collapse and anarchy overwhelm the nation. Armed factions might fight for supremacy, possibly involving other countries in the conflict. Japanese firms would lose their Chinese assets and customers, investors would flee Asia, neighboring countries would arm themselves, and refugees might sail to Japan.

It is questionable though, how much Japan would really be affected by turmoil in China. In all likelihood, Chinese would kill other Chinese rather than attack foreign nations. The southwestern Japanese islands are 600 kilometers from China's coast, too far for Chinese military units to raid Japan. The possible military reaction of China's land neighbors would have little impact on Japan. The economic impact of such a development would be significant, but Japan has weathered worse crises. China, for all its growth, is not a vital cog in the world economy. And it is very doubtful that large numbers of boat people would land on Japan's shores because of the distances involved and Japan's unwelcoming image.

Nevertheless, the perceived risks of fighting in a country with millions of soldiers, nuclear weapons, ballistic missiles, and strong anti-Japanese sentiment can cause anxiety in Japan. Moreover, the Chinese economy is now a market of consequence for Japan. A Chinese collapse would not only affect the PRC itself but also Hong Kong (an economically separate entity from the PRC), Taiwan, and possibly Southeast Asia and Far Eastern Russia. Japanese nationals might be caught in civil disturbances and held hostage. Foreign investors might "red line" Asia. As for Chinese "boat people," Japan is easily alarmed at such possibilities because it has no tradition of accepting refugees.

To prevent such a contingency, Japan has aided China in its quest for economic progress. In the process, it has turned a blind eye to human rights violations, and adopted a low profile during the missile tests near Taiwan in March 1996. Therefore, so far, the paradigm upon which Japan's policy toward China has been based is help for, rather than containment of, China.

If China decided to seek hegemony in Korea, however, it would rapidly become a threat in Japanese eyes. This is because China, though militarily weak, is not without resources to destabilize Korea. The PRC could seek, perhaps successfully, the removal of the USFK by playing on Korean anti-American and anti-Japanese feelings, and on the perceived attractiveness of the Chinese market. China has the advantage of being seen as a friendly nation by some Koreans whereas Japan has a bad image; and since younger South Koreans are more anti-Japanese than their elders, this problem may not end soon.[21] Anti-Americanism is also found in various sectors of South Korean society while some Koreans have a romantic attachment to China and its culture. These factors are unlikely to sway Korea but Chinese maneuvers to gain a foothold in Korea would look very frightening to Japan.

Moreover, the PRC will be able to destabilize united Korea. Regardless of the success of unification, there will be some discontented Koreans, and China will have the tools to manipulate them. In particular, Beijing could subvert Korea by using its links to former North Korean individuals and organizations. It could also use ethnic Koreans in China as infiltrators and agents.

In addition, during the transition toward unification—which has already started—China will be vitally important to South Korea. China can facilitate or hinder the South's goals in North Korea. It can help Seoul by keeping the North from collapsing violently—or make matters worse either by propping up uncooperative elements in Pyongyang or causing the North's fragile economy to crash, thus forcing Seoul to pick up the pieces. Therefore Beijing has far more leverage on South Korea than that exercised by Japan.

Beijing could, furthermore, enlist those Americans with a benign view of its intentions to support the withdrawal of American soldiers from Korea. A worst-case scenario for Japan would be a reversal of American policy priorities—one in which America would move away from Japan and toward Sino-American entente at the cost of the U.S.-Japan relationship.

Finally, if it successfully brought Korea back into its orbit, China could be emboldened enough to try bringing Japan under its influence. Ming China (1368-1644) considered Japan as having been a tributary of China since the Han dynasty (202 BC - 220 AD).[22] At the turn of the fifteenth century, one of the shoguns of Japan, Yoshimitsu, accepted the title "King of Japan" from the Chinese emperor.[23] The Tokugawa Shoguns, however, rejected the title of King of Japan.[24] Throughout most of recorded history thereafter, Japan was on the far outer fringes of the Chinese world order, with the last tribute mission recorded in 1549 while Japan was in the throes of civil war.[25] Still, a really ambitious China could seek, if not a return of Japan to its tributary position, at least the clear establishment of Chinese supremacy in the Asian pecking order.

Some Japanese suspect that the PRC's ultimate goal is to extend its sphere of influence to Korea, Japan, and Southeast Asia.[26] Any Chinese thrust, successful or not, to transform Korea into a satellite would fuel Japanese suspicions. Regardless of the real military impact of such a situation, the psychological effect on Japan would be very powerful. The new generation of Japanese leaders has no experience of the Sino-Japanese War of 1937-1945 and thus no direct guilt feelings about the deeds of the Imperial Japanese Army. Consequently, they are wont to be more assertive with China and less inhibited in following Japan's national interest in a hard-nosed fashion.[27] Moreover, since the demise of the Soviet Union the PRC has lost its usefulness as an objective ally against the Russian menace. All of these factors, combined with the departure of the American forces from Asia and Korea's unification, might foster a massive Japanese arms buildup.

UNIFICATION PROCESS

Korea is subject to strong regional and ideological rivalries. Factional disputes, possibly degenerating into civil disturbances, could accompany or follow unification.

United Korea will not have the same margin for error after unification as Germany enjoyed. Wealth and four decades of peaceful bourgeois democracy cushioned united Germany's mistakes, which have nevertheless cost western Germans hundreds of billions of marks and generated resentment in eastern Germany. South Korea is poorer than West Germany, and lacks a solid tradition of internal stability; at the same time, North Korea is in worse shape than East Germany ever was. Moreover, North Koreans make up 33 percent of the peninsula's total population (versus the 21 percent of East Germans as a percentage of united Germany's citizens). The political union of these two societies, much more dissimilar than were East and West Germany, will be complex. An ineffective economic policy, or just the sheer magnitude of rescuing the North, might end in economic catastrophe. This, in turn, could lead to political unrest.

Such a scenario would create several problems: Japanese exporters would be affected by the collapse of the Korean economy; Koreans might blame Japan for Korea's ills, leading politicians to seek political capital by becoming overtly anti-Japanese; Korean factions could ally with China or Russia. Korean refugees might even reach Japan, in which case Japanese stereotypes about the Korean community could cause fear of subversion or crime in Japan, and breed more Korean-Japanese tensions.

Until Japan vanquished Russia in 1905, Korea's weakness and disunity made it the object of Chinese, Russian, and Japanese rivalry, which in turn resulted in wars and Japan's colonization of the country. A return to the pattern of pre-1905 rivalries would put Japan in a difficult position. It has few cards to play, and operates with the disadvantage of being the party Koreans most dislike.

Economic Reconstruction

North Korea is wretchedly poor. Its citizens have no experience of a market economy. To rehabilitate it, Seoul will need foreign investment and might seek foreign aid.

After unification, Japanese and other foreign manufacturers will have the opportunity to set up factories in North Korea. This foreign investment will be essential in rehabilitating the North. But while Japanese investment will be welcomed for its economic benefits, it will simultaneously create new sources of tension. The sight of Japanese-owned factories could inflame Korean nationalism. South Korea's development has not relied much on foreign investment, and neither North nor South Koreans are used to the massive presence of foreign manufacturers and firms (though the recent agreement with the IMF on foreign investment will help Korea prepare for unification).

Besides investment, aid will also become an issue. Aid is not what united Korea will need most.[28] Foreign investment, better access to foreign markets, and domestic deregulation will be far more useful. In addition, pride may lead Korea to forego foreign assistance.

Nevertheless, it is likely that after unification many policymakers, both in Korea and abroad, will emphasize the importance of foreign aid. Thus, the aid issue will become relevant regardless of economic benefits. Indeed, the dire situation in North Korea may make emergency foreign contributions necessary to avoid a famine and refugee movements.

In other words, there will probably be an aid program. The United States will stress that its military contribution to Korean security for a half-century means that, in the spirit of "burden-sharing," Japan should contribute a disproportionate portion of the economic package. To satisfy Korean sensitivities, the aid package might be described as loans or war reparations from Japan or merged into an international rescue program.

Negotiating this aid deal could lead to disputes between Tokyo and Seoul. Moreover, an aid program for Korea may cause Japanese-American tensions. The U.S. administration may make Japan pay for Korea's reconstruction without giving it much say in regional security policy (during the Gulf War Japan wrote a $13 billion check but had no input into Coalition policies). Such a situation may be unacceptable to the Japanese, and create a new source of friction between Tokyo and Washington.

DEALING WITH CHANGE: OBSTACLES TO JAPANESE SUCCESS ON THE KOREAN PENINSULA

The challenges outlined above are not insurmountable, especially for a nation with the economic and technological strength of Japan. Unfortunately for the Japanese, however, the Japanese government is ill-equipped to face the strategic decisions it will have to make in case of Korean unification, especially if it is rapidly followed by an American withdrawal from Asia. The following pages explain the major obstacles that Japan will confront in its efforts to design and implement a strategy to deal with the new situation.

BILATERAL ALLIANCE WITH THE UNITED STATES

No other major American ally is so exclusively tied to the U.S. as Japan. Germany, Canada, and Britain, among others, have a closer military rapport with the United States, but, unlike Japan, they have meaningful security relations with other allies besides America.

The United States has been the lodestar of Japanese diplomacy and security policy for decades. Japan has practically no experience in dealing with security issues with Korea, China, Taiwan, and Russia. Close ties with Washington and the U.S.-managed regional order have enabled Tokyo to avoid having to manage the regional security environment on its own. In the military field, the SDF cooperate closely with the U.S. military, but are not used to working with other armed forces, though Japanese soldiers have participated in peacekeeping (but not peacemaking) operations.

Those U.S.-Japan ties started during the Occupation, when the primary task of the Ministry of Foreign Affairs was as liaison with the foreign (U.S.) occupation authority.[29] A Japanese academic[30] noted in 1970 that the U.S. is "a constant buffer between our consciousness and reality," and "a cushion between Japan and the realities of war and history." In many ways, this is still the case in 1998. Japan would find it very difficult, therefore, to adjust to a situation in which the United States had retreated from its leading role in Asia. Japan is the greatest Asian economic power, but its civilian and military officials have only a very limited experience in dealing with other Asian nations on security issues. The entire national security apparatus would have to handle countless problems which for the past fifty years have been taken care of by the Americans.

LIMITED MILITARY POWER

Japan's supremacy is economic, not military. The strongest armed forces in the region belong to an outside power, the United States. China has a far larger army (though poorly equipped), a brutal regime with territorial claims on many of its neighbors, strategic depth, a willingness to sacrifice tens of millions of lives, and nuclear weapons. North Korea, besides its million-man military, has a nuclear program (now allegedly "frozen"), ballistic missiles, and a tradition of aggression and covert action against South Korea. Likewise, South Korea and Taiwan have large militaries, and far more trained reservists than Japan. Japan's armed forces are not insignificant, but Japanese military power is still limited. The country's military-industrial base is small. The SDF have neither power projection forces, operational experience overseas, nor a nuclear arsenal. The country only has limited military intelligence capabilities and a small space program. The mainstream Japanese ideology and the country's unfortunate history in 1931-45 make the Japanese government very reluctant to use military power. It has not participated in any military action since 1945, and its officers and men have never undertaken large overseas deployments. The SDF are organized to work in cooperation with U.S. forces rather than alone. For example, its navy is tailored for cooperative missions with its American counterpart and thus is not easily put to use in autonomous action.[31]

Japan's economy makes it a virtual superpower. It could develop a mighty military without risking bankruptcy. It would, however, take years and revolutionary political decisions at the highest level before its military power would be commensurate with its economic weight. The mental outlook of Japan's political class would also have to change radically. As of today Japan's strength depends entirely on economic performance and the U.S. alliance.

GOVERNMENT ORGANIZATION

Korean unification, especially if followed by American withdrawal, will require Japan to play a higher-profile security role than it has for many years. This, however, could overload the government and bureaucracy. One of the effects of Japan's post-World War II situation has been to limit the country's need for, and ability to implement, effective national-security decision-making. Though Japan has sizable armed forces, its institutional capacity to deal with crises is very limited. Japan lacks the political leadership to respond coherently to a new international environment. Moreover, the Japanese civil service suffers from strong internal factionalism between ministries and bureaus, thus preventing bureaucrats from generating an effective policy internally. Consequently, if a major crisis erupted, the Japanese government could find itself rudderless and incapable of making effective and rapid decisions.

The reaction to the Kobe earthquake, for instance, was not impressive for a nation as rich, technologically advanced, and disciplined as Japan. And when Japanese diplomats were taken hostage in Peru, Japan looked feckless; most other G-7 countries, such as the United States, Germany, France, or the UK, would have had an elite rescue team at the ready, but Japan did not. The Prime Minister's office lacks the institutional organization to run national security policy. Furthermore, the prime minister is sometimes barely more than *primus inter pares* and surrounded by powerful political chieftains who limit his ability to make decisions quickly. In the absence of a strong chief executive, each ministry acts on its own in an uncoordinated and counterproductive manner. Because post-1945 Japan has never faced a national security emergency, there has been no need to reform the system for greater efficiency.

Japan's problem in managing national security policy predates 1945. After the post-1868 oligarchs faded away in the early twentieth century, the government never properly coordinated the army, navy, and foreign office. During the crises of the 1930s and 1940s, there was no single individual or entity—be it the monarch, cabinet, or the army and naval staffs—which controlled the national security apparatus. The result was uncoordinated and ineffective strategy. The question in the 1990s, then, is not dangerous militarism or imperialism but a lack of administrative coherence and of a power center to harmonize ministries, agencies, and the armed services. Japan can solve these organizational problems, but it will take time and enormous energy on the part of the government.

POLITICAL CULTURE AND "CONSENSUS"

The popular image of Japan as a conflict-free nation based on consensus is misleading. The myth of Japanese consensus needs to be unmasked because it leads to erroneous views of Japanese policy. In particular, if Korean unification forces Japan to confront difficult choices, major policy cleavages could divide the nation. Because of the strength of Japan's middle class democracy, this would not lead to revolution or civil war but could nevertheless make it difficult for Japan to design and implement an effective national strategy.

The concept of consensus may be relevant to a sociological study of Japanese mores and culture. Consensus-seeking, however, does not explain Japanese political history. In Japan, as in other countries, disputes have often led to violence. In the sixteenth century, following almost a hundred years of civil war, three warlords (Oda Nobunaga, Toyotomi Hideyoshi, and Tokugawa Ieyasu) unified Japan with a Bismarckian blend of blood, iron, and diplomacy. The battle of Sekigahara in 1600 and the siege of the Osaka castle in 1615, rather than any consensual meeting, sealed the victory of the Tokugawas.[32] Afterwards, they confiscated about half of Japan's taxable land from unfriendly provincial daimyo[33] (semi-independent hereditary regional lords). During their long tenure (1603-1868) the Tokugawas jealously upheld their military supremacy, and forced the wives and children of the feudatories to reside as hostages in Edo (now Tokyo).

Acts of violence by Japanese against fellow countrymen marked the collapse of the Tokugawa bakufu (the "tent government," of the shogun) in the 1850s and 1860s. Conspirators liquidated their foes, undermined feudal courts, and murdered foreign residents.[34] Nor was the new regime built on consensus after the imperial forces overthrew the shogun. One of the ruling oligarchs, Saigo Takamori, broke from his colleagues, starting an uprising in 1877 which ended in a battle wherein 18,000 of his followers were killed or wounded. The government later executed some survivors.[35] As Mark Ramseyer and Frances Rosenbluth conclude: "For all the weight of Japan's so-called 'consensus-building' culture, the oligarchs just could not figure out how to get along."[36] Several Meiji officials fell victim to political assassins.[37] In the 1930s assassinations returned to haunt Japanese politics with a vengeance. Self-styled patriots slew "traitors," a label they pinned on opponents of unrestrained expansionism. Assassination became the continuation of politics by other means. In one infamous incident a disgruntled extremist officer, Lieutenant Colonel Aizawa, decapitated General Nagata Tetsuzan in the general's office.

Following World War II, the U.S.-controlled government introduced a new order and politics became far less immoderate. Nevertheless, not all decisions resulted from consensus. First, the new constitution (technically an amendment to the 1889 charter) owed more to the unilateral desires of General Douglas MacArthur than to Japanese consensus. Second, even after the establishment of the new system, some major decisions involved unseemly clashes. In 1960, police entered the Diet chamber to remove Socialist parliamentarians opposed to the U.S.-Japan Security Treaty;[38] and on the occasion of the revisions of education legislation, policemen went into the Upper House of the Diet.[39] Far leftist students in the 1960s were intolerant extremists. They resembled, though without the bloody outcome, the radicals of the Bakumatsu period and the ultra-nationalists of the Showa Restoration.[40] They were more ferocious than their Western counterparts. Their terrorist outgrowth, the Japanese Red Army, was the most fanatical avatar of this global phenomenon, which included the Bader-Meinhof gang, the Red Brigades, and the Weather Underground.[41]

Because Japanese society is often not consensual, disagreements can be as violent as in Western nations. Thus, if Japan's national security policy changes radically, a significant part of the electorate could oppose it rather than create a new consensus. As a result, Japan could become a nation internally fractured between proponents of different national security policies and the nature of its political system might prevent it from implementing any coherent policy.

CONFRONTING THE PAST

The unification of Korea should entail Japan developing new relationships with Korea and possibly China. This will require Japanese society to take a new look at its colonization of Korea and at the wars with China (a matter of immense sensitivity to Koreans and, to a significant extent, Chinese). Koreans consider Japan's failure to condemn its past imperialism unconditionally an ominous sign that Japan will revert to aggression. Many Koreans repeat that as long as Japan does not show contrition for the past, relations are bound to stay unhealthy.

History is a divisive question in Japan. Many Japanese are loath to accept Korean and Chinese views that Imperial Japan committed heinous crimes. Japan suffers from what Ian Buruma diagnosed as "selective historical amnesia."[42] If the government issued West German-like apologies, large segments of society, such as the powerful Bereaved War Families Association, would be greatly upset. A complete atonement for the war and its attendant atrocities would require a critical analysis of the role of the late Showa Emperor (Hirohito), a matter which remains almost taboo.

On the whole, it is unlikely that Japan will deal with its past in a way which will satisfy Korean demands. (West) Germany's experience in confronting the Hitler period has been the exception rather than the rule. "Historical amnesia" has not been limited to Japan, as shown by the unwillingness for many decades of many European nations, such as Austria, France, Italy, Switzerland, and even the Channel Islands, to reflect on their own behavior during World War II. Moreover, even a German-style full apology might not be enough. Fifty-three years and countless apologies, reparations, and symbolic gestures later, Germany's image still suffers greatly from the events of World War II and the Federal Republic's margin of maneuvers in international affairs is still severely constrained by the lingering aftermath of the Nazi era. Thus, the past will continue to be an obstacle to Japan's ability to deal effectively with Korea and China.

Korean unification will put more pressure on Japan to deal with its history because of the need to redefine relations with a united Korea. The result could be increased divisions in Japan between those who put honoring the war dead above all else and those who favor atoning for the past.

Finally the animosities which Imperial Japan's actions have generated in Asia make it difficult for Japan to strengthen its military because any increase in Japanese military power, even if totally justified, will be viewed as a resurgence of imperialism. Any attempt by Japan to become more powerful militarily, then, might be counterproductive since it could only encourage further anti-Japanese policies on the Asian mainland.

ANTIMILITARISM

During the 1930s and throughout World War II, the Japanese uniformed services and their generals and admirals dominated policymaking—a situation much different from that of Nazi Germany and Fascist Italy, where policymaking had fallen into the possession of civilian murderers with the military confined to implementing their decisions. Consequently, the Japanese military received most of the blame for the War,[43] especially because MacArthur and subsequent Japanese governments cleared the Showa Emperor of responsibility.[44] The war engendered a "culture of anti-militarism,"[45] and many Japanese reached the conclusion that armed forces are evil regardless of circumstances. The use by postwar Japanese governments of pacifist rhetoric has also contributed to the antimilitarist climate.

Consider, as an example of Japan's mistrust of the armed services, what occurred in the country during the Gulf War. "The Kaifu government deliberately excluded Defense Agency personnel from reporting directly to the cabinet," since it feared that the military would influence the decisions of individual cabinet members.[46] As a result, the defense establishment was not involved in discussions of a major national security issue.

The reluctance to accept military power as an essential part of national security policy is visible within the defense debate. For example, the prestigious Institute for International Policy Studies' report on a "Comprehensive Strategy for Japan" devoted almost as much space to discussing the building of a new capital for Japan as to national security policy guidelines.[47] The SDF itself emphasizes its contribution to natural disaster relief and other nonmilitary contingencies to justify its existence.

The interest-group nature of Japanese politics has reinforced the impact of antimilitarism. As Kent Calder wrote in *Crisis and Compensation,* the "compensation-oriented cast" of Japanese policymaking makes defense a "residual [rather] than a strategic priority"[48]—especially unattractive because there is little "pork" in it.[49] The SDF have few members compared to the millions of small businessmen, farmers, and other traditional constituent groups. Moreover, the largest SDF contractors are civilian enterprises for whom defense is only a small percentage of their revenues.[50] The combination of idealist antimilitarism and pork barrel politics severely restricts Japan's military effort.

As a result of antimilitarism in large segments of the population, the government finds it difficult to initiate policies which would barely raise an eyebrow in most other countries. For instance, when the SDF deploys Japanese peacekeepers abroad, debates break out as to whether they may carry machine guns; even small contributions to UN operations ignite suspicion of resurgent "militarism." In this way, antimilitarism curtails the government's freedom of action in making national security policy.

FEELINGS OF VULNERABILITY

Unlike that of the United States within North America and the Caribbean littoral, Japan's demographic weight is small within its region. Only 8.6 percent of Northeast Asians are Japanese. For every Japanese there are almost ten Chinese nationals. Japan is also twenty-five times smaller than China and only 1.7 times larger than South and North Korea combined. Its densely populated areas around Tokyo and Osaka make it particularly vulnerable to a few weapons of mass destruction. This comparatively small population and geographic base partly explain Japanese insecurity.

Japan is in an awkward situation. Its neighbors are impressed by, and often fearful of, its strength. They see a country which produces almost three quarters of Northeast Asia's wealth and once controlled a "Co-Prosperity Sphere" from Sumatra to the Kuriles. The Japanese, by contrast, see a small island devoid of resources and without local allies. This contrast between Japanese and Asian views of Japan makes Japanese policymaking and relations with Asia even more difficult to manage.

JAPAN'S ISOLATION IN THE WORLD

To manage international security issues a country needs to be adept at dealing with foreign nations. For historical and cultural reasons, Japan is isolated from the rest of the world; consequently, its expertise at dealing with foreign countries is limited. For all its economic weight,

Japan is still on the periphery of the international community. As Bill Emmott of *The Economist* realized, for the Japanese there exists "[a] strange world outside."[51]

There are no countries to which Japan is culturally close in the way that Italy and Canada or Australia and Germany can claim closeness as the result of belonging to the same civilization. Korea, Taiwan, and China, the three countries which most resemble Japan, are in fact very different, culturally, politically, and economically.

Moreover, because it is an island, Japan is geographically cut off from other nations. It has had very limited foreign relations with the rest of the world for most of its recorded history. In the 1630s, the shogunate closed the country, banning virtually all travel and commerce to and from Japan for over two centuries. After its "opening" in the 1850s, Japan's intercourse with other nations remained circumscribed by distance and politics.

Cultural Isolation. Of the rich non-Western capitalist societies, Japan is the most culturally detached from the West. Britain gave Hong Kong and Singapore a strong dose of Western influence; and education and migration to America have resulted in the elites of Taiwan and South Korea becoming more familiar with Western culture than their Japanese counterparts. Of course, knowledge of Western mores does not imply that Taiwanese or South Koreans have mutated into Westerners, but they are better able to function in a Western environment.

In addition, Japan does not belong to the Chinese-speaking world, which connects Chinese, Taiwanese, Hong Kongers, and Singaporean-Chinese with each other and with ethnic Chinese in the West and Asia. And while Koreans benefit from a successful and widely distributed Korean-American community, Japanese-Americans are concentrated in Hawaii and California, and are often third or fourth generation Americans with few ties to Asia. Christianity, which lies at the heart of Western civilization, made fewer inroads in Japan than in other rich Asian societies, especially Korea. Moreover, because Japan has far more people than South Korea or Taiwan, the Japanese market for publications and journals is bigger, so that the need to rely on foreign (mostly Western) books and periodicals is not as great in Japan as elsewhere in Asia. (There are far more Chinese than Japanese, but poverty limits the size of the Chinese market for sophisticated written materials.)

In many ways Japan is as isolated from Asia as it is from the West. The great influx of civilization from China and Korea into Japan stopped centuries ago. Today's Japan has little in common with continental Asia.

There is far more knowledge in Japan of the United States than of contemporary China and Korea. For their part, Chinese and Koreans are more familiar with the West than with Japan. East Asians who study overseas are far more likely to attend Western universities than to go to schools in other Asian nations. Korean, Chinese, and Taiwanese universities use the works of American scholars far more than do those of Japanese schools. Except for classical Chinese texts, Japanese students are exposed to Western authors rather than Chinese or Korean ones. Since 1945, migratory flows have been far larger between East Asian countries and the West than between Asian nations.

Furthermore, Japan's brief colonial experience in Asia did not bind Asia to Japan. The longest period of overseas Japanese rule, on Taiwan, lasted only half a century. Japan's empire incorporated only a few nearby territories (Taiwan, Korea, and, briefly and de facto, Manchukuo) as well as underpopulated German Pacific islands received in mandate from the League of Nations after World War I. Since 1945, the links between these territories and Japan have been far less tight than those between Europe and its former colonies and Europe. Nor did the Japanese put down roots overseas. New Japan, unlike New England or New Spain, never emerged.

Japan's history, geography and culture, and its insularity, reduce opportunities for the country to expand its international profile because they exclude the Japanese from many transnational organizations which allow diplomats and leaders of civil society to interact with their foreign counterparts. These associations are as diverse as regional free-trade agreements, the Commonwealth, the Catholic Church, the associations of Arabic, French, Spanish, or Portuguese-speaking nations, and riverine groups. They generally have no, or very few, Japanese participants. Even Japan's national sport, sumo, is unique to the archipelago. And except for isolated Korean and Chinese communities, unskilled workers, and isolated expatriate executives, Japan has few immigrants who could bring external influences into the country. The Japanese themselves have stopped emigrating from Japan, further limiting ties with the outside world.

The Japanese generate a greater share of the world's wealth than any other language group except English-speakers (i.e., when countries are aggregated by language, no group of nations except the anglophone one has a combined GDP larger than Japan's). Yet Japanese is not an official language of any international agency, nor is it much used in business or science. At the same time, the Japanese school system is bad at teaching foreign languages. Hence, Japanese are less effective at communicating with outsiders than other Asians.

But if Japan is isolated from other societies, the rest of the world is likewise ignorant of things Japanese. For all practical purposes, only Japanese read Japanese newspapers and books. The audience for Japanese satellite TV broadcast is circumscribed to a few other countries. No Japanese media conglomerate has the worldwide reach of Reuters, Pearson, News Corporation, Dow Jones, or Time-Warner/CNN. There are few foreign students in Japan compared to the country's importance, and not many Japanese professors teach overseas. Except for older Taiwanese and Koreans, the number of foreigners capable of conducting a complex discussion in Japanese or of writing an article in that language is minuscule. For various reasons, Japan also does not attract many foreign tourists relative to its size.[52]

Diplomatic Isolation. Japan has a low profile in international organizations, and Japanese nationals are under-represented in international institutions. For example, there are only 141 Japanese on the UN staff, as opposed to 205 Germans, even though Japan has a far larger population and economy and joined the UN decades before Germany.[54] The leading role played by a Japanese UN official in the war in former Yugoslavia was a rare exception. Japanese citizens only head two international agencies, the World Health Organization (WHO) and the UN High Commission for Refugees (UNHCR). No international institution of any importance is headquartered in Japan and Tokyo is rarely the site of international political or scientific conferences, summit meetings, or treaty signings. No Japanese has ever held the Secretary Generalship of the United Nations. The practice of reserving the Managing Directorship of the International Monetary Fund for Europeans and the presidency of the World Bank to U.S. citizens bans Japanese from running these institutions, even though Japan is the second largest shareholder in both. Japan is not a permanent member of the UN Security Council, though it has a larger GDP than four out of the five permanent members, is more populated than two of them, and pays the largest share of the UN's peacekeeping bill.[53]

The Japanese were not as intensely involved in the Cold War as West Europeans and Americans. Because of the absence of a land border with the communists, Japan was not on the ground frontline (although Soviet forces were near Japan, this was not equivalent to the threat posed by the Warsaw Pact armies to Europe). As a result, the U.S. military presence in Japan during the Cold War was small compared to the numbers of troops stationed in Europe. Moreover, there was no need for Washington to organize a massive multilateral military presence in Japan as it did in Germany after the war. American and NATO European officers have had far more experience interacting with foreigners through working and training abroad than have their Japanese counterparts.

Today, the Japanese armed forces are only marginally involved in international peacekeeping operations (approximately forty-five Japanese soldiers are stationed on the Golan Heights). Japanese defense industry does participate in a few collaborative armaments projects with the United States. It is, however, insular compared to its European and American counterparts, for whom international programs are the norm. Japan's restrictions on arms exports further curb its involvement in security affairs. Japanese defense contractors and military personnel do not train foreign militaries or travel overseas to maintain equipment and negotiate sales. Except for U.S. equipment, Japan buys almost no foreign defense hardware.

Japan was also on the sidelines during the ideological Cold War. After 1945, Japan's government was not particularly interested in the global fight against the Red Menace,[54] and the ideological component of the Cold War played a lesser role in Japan than in the Atlantic world. Korea and China were geographically divided between communist and right-wing governments. Consequently, in South Korea and the Republic of China (Taiwan) there was a massive ideological indoctrination of the citizenry until the collapse of Soviet communism and the relative deténte with the PRC (and, to a lesser extent, North Korea). In Japan, however, there was no such overwhelming drive on the part of conservatives to fight international communism. The Communist party did not have a power comparable to its largest West European counterparts, nor was there a communist half of the country. No Japanese politician or writer played a prominent international role in countering communist philosophy (nor, for that matter, did any Japanese Marxist attain international stature). Prime Minister Nakasone was an important world leader in the 1980s, but unlike his conservative contemporaries, Ronald Reagan, John Paul II, and Margaret Thatcher, his name is not associated with ideological and philosophical attacks on Marxism.

Isolation in the Business World. The top echelons of Japan's corporate world are almost exclusively Japanese. Most leading North American, European, and Southeast Asian corporations have senior staffers from foreign countries. Foreign-born executives run Ford, Deutsche Telekom, L'Oréal, and Stanford University; but CEOs of large Japanese companies always come from Japan itself (Mazda was an exception because its largest shareholder is American). Japan has no genuine transnational company, that is, one whose management is as international as its markets. Furthermore, foreign investment has played a less important role in Japan than in Europe,[55] so the influx of foreign companies, managers, and products has been more limited in Japan than in Europe. Conversely, non-Japanese multinational firms rarely have managers from Japan, further isolating Japan's business class.

Japan's profile in world affairs has grown since the 1960s. The time when the Japanese prime minister could be dismissed as a mere "transistor salesman" are gone.[56] Nevertheless, Japan's history and political organization still limit its ability to respond effectively to major crises and changes in the regional order. Consequently, the unification of Korea and ensuing changes in the region could become a formidable challenge for Japan.

CHAPTER FOUR
CHINA[1]

Korean unification could undermine the peaceful environment on which China's security and prosperity depend. It could also foster tensions with Korea, and more ominously, with Japan and the United States—a situation that might well wreck the international trade and investment climate China needs to continue developing economically. It may also foreshadow a military competition with Japan, and perhaps America, which it cannot win.

In spite of its failure to expel the United States from Korea during the Korean War,[2] China has adapted well to the Korean stalemate. During the Sino-Soviet confrontation, American soldiers in Korea and Japan helped China by providing a counterweight to Soviet power. Since the détente between Moscow and Beijing, the division of Korea has continued to serve China. South Korea has become a trading and investment partner while North Korea is a useful buffer between China and the capitalist world. The American troops, separated from China by North Korea, have maintained East Asian peace. Once Korea is united, however, this advantageous status quo will be at risk.

On one hand, Korean unification will weaken the Chinese Communist party because it will mark the first collapse of an East Asian communist regime.[3] It may thus contribute to the demise of the People's Republic.

On the other hand, Korean unification will give China opportunities to enhance its stature, by establishing a stronger position in Korea, but may turn out to be a trap because it could generate strong anti-Chinese reactions in Korea, Japan, Russia, and the United States.

RELATIONS WITH KOREA

Sino-Korean relations are not as emotionally charged as those between China and Japan. In spite of the intervention of the PLA[4] in the Korean war, South Koreans are well-inclined toward China. On the Chinese side, there appears to be little animosity against Koreans, and the Chinese are impressed by South Korea's economic miracle. Unification will, however, multiply the chances of friction and tensions between Beijing and Seoul.

Ethnic Koreans. There are an estimated two million Chinese nationals of Korean ancestry living in Jilin province near North Korea.[5] The Korean-Chinese have done well. The Han Chinese consider them a "model minority,"[6] and admire for them for their hard work and educational achievements. They are the only minority with a higher socio-educational level than the Han themselves. In addition, there are Korean-Chinese in the top echelons of the Chinese state, including the army. Unlike Tibetans and Xinjiang Turkic Moslems, they have not been agitating against Beijing's authority.

Until the normalization of South Korean-PRC relations, which started in the 1980s and was formalized in 1992, Korean-Chinese had no links with the ROK. In the past decade, however, contacts have grown between South Korea and China, and therefore between Korean-Chinese and South Koreans and Korean-Americans. Many Korean-Chinese work in South Korean business ventures in China, as well as in ROK diplomatic missions in China as clerical staffers. In brief, the Korean-Chinese are emerging from isolation and establishing ties with their co-ethnics on the peninsula.

The potential for "re-Koreanization" of Chinese citizens of Korean descent, who are rediscovering their Korean heritage, is a problem for the PRC. Some Chinese reported with concern that, during the 1988 Seoul Olympics, ethnic Korean-Chinese cheered South Korean athletes. Korean-American and South Korean missionaries have also proselytized the Christian gospel to Korean-Chinese, who have become active in Beijing's fledgling Christian community. Christianity has been very successful in South Korea (16.3 percent are Protestant, and 4.8 percent Catholic,[7] the only large Christian community[8] in a nation which Westerners never colonized), and Christians have played leading roles in democratization. Not surprisingly, the PRC authorities are concerned by this religious activity, especially because Christians have strong ties with the West. Moreover, South Korea is richer and freer than China and thus a dangerous magnet for China's ethnic Koreans.

It is possible that once Korea is unified, ethnic Koreans could gravitate towards Korea. Contacts and investments from Korea will further push South Korean influence northward into China. Deng's reforms have weakened the power of the party and state in China, making the country more vulnerable to economic, cultural, and demographic penetration from outside powers. Because of the xenophobic and dictatorial nature of the Chinese regime, the growing

Korean presence in Korean-Chinese area will worry the Chinese government and create friction with Korea.

The Korean-Chinese are less than 0.2 percent of the Chinese population, and although their district is not large, they inhabit a strategic area. They are close to the southern part of the Russian Maritime Provinces (next to North Korea), which China may covet to gain access to the Sea of Japan if the Russian Federation grows weaker.[9] Moreover, because the Korean-Chinese region is on a foreign border, it is a more sensitive zone than if it were a remote landlocked province of the PRC.

Territorial and Maritime Issues. Controversies have already arisen between Beijing and Seoul over the demarcation of maritime boundaries for fishing and oil exploration rights. Once the ROK's authority is extended to present-day North Korea, the scope for maritime and border disagreements will increase considerably because the ROK and China will share a land border and a longer maritime and airspace boundary. China and Korea take hard-line views of their sovereignty, and thus the disputes could take a nasty turn.

Additionally, in ancient times, areas of northern China were part of Korea, and there are a few Koreans who consider these lands, especially because of their ethnic Koreans inhabitants, as part of a "Greater Korea." Korea will not claim Manchuria. But a feeling of suspicion in China about Korean intentions could worsen Sino-Korean relations.

Asymmetric relations. China will probably want Korea to enter into a tributary relationship because Beijing will not see the relationship as one of equals, if only because of China's size and the historical background of Sino-Korean intercourse. For its part, a "big brother-little brother" relationship will be unacceptable to Korea and will create tensions between the two countries.

U.S. FORCES IN NORTHEAST ASIA

If U.S. military forces remain in Korea in the post-unification period, the United States will have servicemen in a country contiguous to China for the first time in the PRC's history. This will disturb the communist leadership and also thwart Chinese dreams of bringing Korea into its orbit. Even if American units do not deploy into the former North Korea, U.S. soldiers in a country whose northern half used to be part of the communist world will be an ominous signal for Chinese communists. All of these factors will push the communist regime to seek the removal of U.S. forces from Korea.

Their departure, however, would be dangerous for China. Officially Beijing will welcome the end of the American presence on the Asian mainland. On the other hand, as noted earlier, great (and middle) power rivalries will resurface in Northeast Asia as soon as upholders of the *pax americana*. This in turn will lead to instability in the region and derail China's economic development.

U.S. withdrawal from Korea and Asia after Korean unification is possible. After unification, the United States might wish to further reduce military spending by cutting its forces on the Korean peninsula and in Japan. At the same time, China might support Koreans, Japanese, and Americans who oppose U.S. military presence.

Chinese opposition to America's Asian policies could lead to severe strains between the United States and China, especially if China engages in aggressive behavior such as active support for anti-U.S. elements in Korea, military operations in the Taiwan Straits and the South China Sea, and more human rights violations. The emergence of the U.S. as a foe of the Chinese regime would be a serious reversal for China. The United States cannot invade China, but a truly hostile America would be devastating for Beijing because the United States leads alliances and treaties (NATO, U.S.-Japan, U.S.-ROK, ANZUS) which encompass all the world's rich nations. U.S. influence over the G-7, WTO, the OECD, the IMF, and the World Bank is great, and though the United States cannot dictate policies to its allies, it can influence them significantly. Through legislative and diplomatic moves the United States can throttle the Chinese economy (the U.S. sanctions after the Tiananmen Square massacre had no effect because the U.S. government was ambivalent and did not wish to confront the Chinese and thus only imposed very mild measures).

China is a big market for foreign businesses, but far smaller than that of the United States (in fact Chinese GDP is smaller than California's). Therefore, if America restricted investment and trade with the PRC, as well as curtailed educational exchanges, travel, and other links, China would suffer greatly. Many foreign companies would scale down or abandon their Chinese operations to avoid American sanctions. And the end of U.S. investment and China's inability to establish normal economic relations with the United States would be a major blow. Even selective sanctions, such as the ones applied against the USSR after the invasion of Afghanistan, could be a severe impediment. In several key industries such as oil, aerospace, and software, there is a significant cost to be paid for being on the U.S. "hit list" because American corporations dominate these sectors.

Moreover, the United States can subvert the Chinese regime. America's links with Taiwan and the presence of many PRC Chinese in America give the United States powerful tools against Beijing. The U.S. could use its large contingent of PRC Chinese residents and Chinese-Americans to organize covert operations and sponsor political dissent. It could finance dissident groups and organize anti-CCP media abroad. It could also recruit PRC Chinese studying or working in America to conspire against their government, making returnees suspect in the eyes of the Communist party. American agencies could also support, in alliance with other countries, agitators and subversive elements from China's ethnic minorities.

As of today, China has nothing to fear militarily from Japan. The SDF have no offensive capability, and postwar Japan has eschewed force in the conduct of diplomacy. But if the U.S. withdraws from East Asia after the unification of Korea, Japan is likely to enhance its military power greatly, especially if China attempts to seek hegemony in Korea. Because of Japan's historical baggage and China's own politics, a Japan with a large military will alarm Beijing.

Moreover, Japanese investment and trade is very important for China's economic growth. Were Japan to impose economic sanctions on China, China's economic development would suffer, especially if these were applied in conjunction with the United States.

IMPLICATIONS FOR CHINESE POLITICS

The PRC and North Korea are very different communist societies. Nevertheless, the demise of the DPRK and the victory of the ROK will be a shock for the Chinese leadership. It will show that the collapse of communism, previously limited to Europe, can occur in Asia (the Mongolian and Afghan communist regimes were special cases because they were creatures of the Soviet Union). The demise of Korean communism could embolden more Chinese to question Communist party rule at home. It may also divide the Chinese leaders. Some might argue that to survive they must reform China even more rapidly; others could call for a return to orthodoxy to save the party from catastrophe.

Korean unification will thus have a negative impact on the Communist party's ability to rule China. The CCP will be unable to insulate China from the consequences of the destruction of an East Asian communist regime for which China went to war in 1950. It will have to explain to the masses why North Korea has disappeared. It will meet more difficulties in pressing its claim that Taiwan, a country quite similar to South Korea, should submit to Beijing's rule.

OVERCOMING THE CHALLENGES OF KOREAN UNIFICATION

Weaker than the United States and Japan, China faces an uncertain future. Beijing will thus find it difficult to deal effectively with the challenges arising from Korean unification because it faces challenges of economic and social transformation. Instability is a more likely scenario than the peaceful evolution of the current regime. In China there has always been only a "relatively thin line between order and chaos."[10] The communist regime resembles the Qing dynasty in its waning years. The Qing empire was "strong enough to cling to tradition and suppress rebellion, yet too weak to provide leadership for change" and its agony (in spite of industrial progress) ended with its overthrow in 1911, followed by decades of turmoil.[11]

Socio-Economic Problems and Stability. Chinese society could soon be rocked by revolutionary upheavals for reasons explained below. Should this happen, the government could find itself largely ineffective in dealing with foreign affairs, provoking it to follow irresponsible policies or leave it unable to react to developments abroad.

As Arthur Waldron notes, economic growth, urban migrations of peasants, and the increase in mass education have rocked Europe in the past; the same process may soon take place in China.[12] The move to the cities, for example, is creating a "mushrooming urban population [that] is going to place an unimaginable burden" on the country's infrastructure.[13] Furthermore, stable polities, such as Britain, survived industrialization relatively peacefully because they had institutions that enjoyed legitimacy and flexibility. In China, by contrast, the Communist party has no moral mandate to rule. It cannot take advantage of the traditional symbols of monarchy and church which European governments could invoke. In the words of a Chinese scholar from Taiwan (in no way antagonistic toward the mainland), China is now "a land of no faith" where only money matters.[14] The regime is vulnerable to an economic downturn, even a temporary one, since such a reversal would lead those who only support it because their income has risen to stop supporting the regime. At a time when people are developing rising expectations, citizens will be enraged if their material conditions stop improving. If, for example, tens of millions of peasants who have moved to the cities lose their jobs because of a recession or a restructuring of state-owned enterprises, the political consequences could be momentous because many of the institutions which gave the regime its iron grip over the populace in the past have decayed.

Corruption further undermines the regime's legitimacy. Officials' self-enrichment scams make most Chinese feel that the system is unfair.

Because communists preached equality, great wealth is more shocking than in "traditional" societies where inequality is seen as natural. The combination of arbitrary bureaucratic power and a liberalized economy provides officials increasing opportunities for corruption and thus can fuel more popular discontent as well as intra-elite rivalries for the loot. Besides making the people unhappy, the rapacious behavior of rent-seeking local governments is driving some Chinese entities to keep their financial reserves overseas to avoid these predators.[15]

The only remaining source of legitimacy will be aggressive nationalism. Because nationalism is generally xenophobic, it would trigger protectionism and less foreign investment and thus stymie economic progress. Nationalism can also lead to antigovernment riots and instability, which is why Beijing has sought to prevent popular expressions of anti-Japanese nationalism over the Senkaku dispute. Popular discontent with inequality can also lead the government to keep many communist practices (such as some state enterprises) in place to mollify the populace, a policy which would also hurt the economy.

The management of the economy is also an enormous challenge. The regime can jail dissidents, but is "unable to systematically collect taxes."[16] State-owned enterprises lose money but employ maybe ninety million or more workers, who represent the bulk of the urban working class. To put these businesses on a market-footing would render these workers jobless, but keeping them afloat drains the banking sector.[17]

Political Stability. Threats to stability may also come from the top. The Chinese political system has never properly institutionalized transfers of power. China has a multimillenarian bureaucracy, but at its apex it is a "lawless"[18] system with "no established process of leadership succession."[19] Besides, "China's crude mechanics of succession and political struggle have hardly changed."[20] Every transition period is fraught with danger because the costs of tolerance of dissent and opposition to the regime are high. Losers are typically disgraced, exiled, jailed, or (in the recent past) slaughtered. This system breeds violence and conspiracy rather than cooperation. The lack of an institutionalized leadership succession at the top of the political pyramid has, in the past, plagued other Asian states; but, in those countries, it was cured by remedies that are not available to China. Japan solved this problem after 1945, thanks to an effective constitution drafted under the American occupation. In South Korea, the presence of the American army ensured that infighting was unlikely to degenerate into civil war. In Taiwan, the danger of PRC intervention induced all Taiwanese to behave with restraint. Moreover, the quasi-institutionalized Chiang dynasty provided stability into the 1980s. The peaceful post-Deng transition indicates that China has resolved this problem for the present, but there is no indication of how long this period of stability will last.

Besides power struggles within the party, China is also vulnerable because of the poor state of the party itself. The CCP is the backbone of the People's Republic. Today, however, it suffers from corruption and the bankruptcy of its ideology. Organizations previously under the party's iron grip, such as the army and the National People's Congress, may be gaining autonomy.[21] The party center is losing its dominion over the economy, society, and regional governments. Yet, though the CCP is "in disrepair," no other institutions have emerged to replace it[22] because it has eradicated competitors to the party's monopoly in politics, economics, and social organizations. The repression of dissidents demonstrates the will of the party to cling to power with a vengeance rather than accept new political actors, as the Kuomintang did in Taiwan. The combination of a decaying party and the lack of institutions with which to replace it is a recipe for instability.

No Stable and Strong Alternative to the CCP. Ten years from now— or even sooner—a different regime may well replace the People's Republic. Regardless of the system which emerges from the overthrow of the Communist party, however, China will remain weak.

A revolution could free the society from the inefficiencies of the old regime and make the country more powerful. This occurred in France in the revolutionary and Napoleonic periods, and in Japan with the Meiji reformation. Louis XVI's France, however, was a modern country with some of Europe's best institutions. The revolutionaries and Bonaparte built on firm ground. Tokugawa Japan was also a strong state; it was pre-industrial but modern in many ways. The shogunate's socio-political base provided a reliable foundation for the Meiji reformers. China has none of these advantages. The emergence of a modern economy after a new revolution would, at best, take many decades. At worst, a revolution could lead to civil war and destruction. The leadership of a political genius might make a difference, but even an extraordinary leader's abilities are constrained by structural conditions inherited from the past.

Some observers think that the overseas Chinese, with their skills and talents, will help China leapfrog several stages of development. The overseas Chinese, however, cannot propel the country into modernity. Their participation in China's development also aggravates regional disparities because most of them are from the coastal south. Moreover, in many cases overseas Chinese investment from other Asian countries has reinforced the corrupt and arbitrary tendencies of China's rulers rather than brought law-based business practices.

Western Influences. China cannot absorb as much from the West as have the smaller Asian nations, but the capitalist world will destabilize the PRC. Thanks to new communications media, more Chinese are gaining a political awareness traditionally forbidden by the regime. Autocrats in South Korea and Taiwan were spared satellite television, and at the time those nations' intellectuals and agitators had no fax machines, PCs, electronic mail, and cellular telephones. Restricting modern technology would, however, slow the Chinese economy, because these instruments are simultaneously the tools of agitators and of business. Myanmar (Burmese) officials can ban modems and fax machines. A country with China's economic ambitions, however, cannot do so without losing all hopes of economic (and thus military) might.

Additionally, the United States, the world's single superpower, is an implacable ideological foe—not because of anything the U.S. government does but because of what America is, i.e., a country whose ethos is in antinomy to PRC ideology and practice. Regardless of U.S. policy toward Beijing, the values of American civilization itself are subversive for the Chinese leadership. The estimated 110,000 PRC students in the United States[23] add to the corrosive impact of America on the Chinese regime. At the same time, to ban students from going to the United States would cut China off from the largest source of the technological and scientific knowledge it needs to modernize its economy.

In the nineteenth century, the Western cultural onslaught traumatized China. Western nations and Japan were the training ground of many Chinese revolutionaries, including Sun Yat-sen and Zhou Enlai. Christianity (with "Chinese characteristics") provided one of the ideological underpinnings of the Taiping rebellion of 1850-1864. Later, other Western ideas, including Marxism, undermined China's traditional political culture. As in the nineteenth century, Western influence will not be sufficient to transform China successfully but will help bring disorder and turmoil to the country.

Ethnic Issues. Another source of instability is ethnic nationalism. The nineteenth century brought China into contact with modern, ethnically-based nationalism. The empire had not been based on an ethnic concept of Chineseness. A man familiar with the classics was civilized, others were barbarians. A non-Chinese who mastered Chinese civilization could rise to senior positions, provided that he conformed to Chinese norms (some European Jesuits achieved very high office in Imperial China; the Qing and Yuan rulers themselves were not Han Chinese). But as nationalism developed and feelings began running high against Westerners, Japanese, and the Manchu rulers, it became clear that not all inhabitants of China were Chinese (defined as Han Chinese). The Han Chinese constitute the vast majority of the population, but the non-Han inhabit large areas which could be separated from China since they are on the country's borders—namely Inner Mongolia, Xinjiang, and Tibet.[24]

China has more ethnic cohesion than the former Soviet Union— the Han Chinese comprise about 93 percent of the citizenry—but because most of the minority areas (e.g., Tibet, Xinjiang, Inner Mongolia) are thinly populated, they cover about 40 percent of the land mass. Japan, Korea, and Taiwan have been spared this problem. Taiwan, for instance, has a Taiwanese-mainlander split, but this division has no territorial dimension and has been mitigated by intermarriage and cross-assimilation. Koreans have strong regional loyalties but no groups which consider themselves separate or advocate secession. Therefore China is much more vulnerable to ethnic separatism than the other Asian states.

Such ethnic issues have international ramifications. In Xinjiang and Inner Mongolia, the co-ethnics of China's non-Han citizens inhabit poor and weak nations (Central Asian republics and Mongolia). These countries pose no military threat to China, but they can internationalize the Xinjiang and Inner Mongolian question. In addition, the Central Asian states' internal weakness can be a danger for China because drug trafficking, organized crime, and smuggling (common in these areas) can undermine Chinese authority in its western territories. In Tibet, the exiled Dalai Lama has internationalized the Tibetan question, thanks to his travel abroad and the respect with which he is held in many foreign capitals. The religious aspect of the Tibet issue has contributed to making it an international question rather than a "Chinese internal affair," as the PRC would like. In the United States, in particular, the great importance given to religious freedom means that even a pro-Beijing administration cannot fail to take the Dalai Lama into account.

Hong Kong. Hong Kong poses two kinds of threats to the PRC. First, it is a free society. As links increase between Hong Kong and China, there will be increasing opportunities for Hong Kong's values to spread to the PRC. Beijing will curtail Hong Kong's liberties, but even a less open Hong Kong will retain some of the mores of a free society for many years. It is, and will remain, a potent conduit for the transmission of subversive thoughts and values into the mainland. In addition, Hong Kong harbors a large foreign community and includes many Chinese who were educated abroad and hold foreign passports. Therefore, enforcing a communist dictatorship in Hong Kong will be more difficult for the Chinese government.

The second problem for Beijing is that, in tandem with Canton (Guangzhou), Hong Kong can foster the growth of uncontrolled Cantonese regionalism. The government has already made efforts to ensure that Hong Kong will come under Beijing's control, bypassing the Cantonese.[25] Nevertheless, it is not clear how successful Beijing will be in curtailing southern autonomy, especially if it wishes to avoid thwarting southern entrepreneurship.

Regionalism. The problem with Hong Kong is only one aspect of Beijing's conflict with regionalism. Many businessmen say that the central government already has only limited control over the rest of the country. The ability of China, however, to establish peacefully a form of regional autonomy, such as the one found in Switzerland or Canada, is doubtful. China's history has, so far, been one of violent fragmentation or unitary rule under dictators. This fact, combined with nationalist pressures in Tibet, Xinjiang, and Inner Mongolia, bodes ill for China's ability to avoid fragmentation. The recent history of the Soviet Union, the Russian Federation, Georgia, Moldova, Tajikistan, Azerbaijan, Afghanistan, Yugoslavia, Bosnia, Czechoslovakia, and Ethiopia indicates how difficult it is for nations with multiple ethnic and regional identities to remain in one piece after the fall of communism.

ECONOMIC FUTURE

In recent years, China's economic progress since the late 1970s has made analysts think that the twenty-first century will belong to China. The past performance of the Chinese economy, however, is not a good indicator of its future prospects.

When Mao Zedong died in 1976, China had reached the nadir of civilization. During the Great Leap Forward of 1958-59, Mao's blindly ambitious schemes killed perhaps forty million individuals. A few years later he unleashed the Cultural Revolution, and "[c]annibalism became a political ritual through which mad mobs maintained their solidarity,"[26] while "rebellion had turned into mob activity in which the students took delight in torturing their teachers and school administrators."[27] Judged by these norms, today's China is a prodigious improvement over the past. The standard of living is higher and growing, there is more freedom, and in light of China's economic growth rate, observers have concluded that "China will overtake the United States as the world's largest economy sometime in the next 25-30 years."[28] Lee Kwan-yew, Singapore's Senior Minister, noted a few years ago that, "I ask myself . . . whether China's growth as a global power can be stopped. I believe it cannot."[29]

These observers assume that China will imitate the economic trajectory of Taiwan and South Korea. They believe that the PRC is comparable to the South Korea and Taiwan of a few decades ago, and that China is progressing on the road of Asian authoritarianism which leads to further economic growth.[30] This prospect appears logical. Taiwan is formally a Chinese province, and its people are of Chinese ancestry. Korea was greatly influenced by China, and for centuries its elite was steeped in the Chinese classics. Moreover, like the People's Republic, both Taiwan and South Korea grew economically without the benefit of democracy. In the nineteenth century, Japan likewise became a power of consequence under authoritarian samurai-politicians.

One must, however, distinguish between decaying communism in the People's Republic of China and semi-capitalist authoritarianism (Meiji Japan; Taiwan, and South Korea prior to democratization). Besides, between China on the one hand and Taiwan, Korea, and Japan on the other, there are various differences which limit the relevance of their experience in predicting China's future.

China's GDP has grown rapidly in recent decades, partly because by the end of the Cultural Revolution the nation's economy was in shambles. Just as an explorer standing on the South Pole can walk northwards without good navigational skills, China's economic performance could only improve after Mao because almost any other policy would have been better. Deng Xiaoping's reforms, however, will not ensure continued success. Removing barriers to economic activity quickly stimulated growth, even without the institutions of capitalism, because small-scale repeat exchanges in homogenous cultures (for example, Chinese farmers bartering pigs and rice) need little institutionalized enforcement such as laws, judges, and honest policemen.[31] Furthermore, when liberalization began in the late 1970s, 71 percent of workers were in agriculture, "a sector long crippled by artificially low prices and poor productivity" where reforms quickly lifted productivity.[32] In addition, China's huge population, low wages, and the ethnic Chinese diaspora facilitated foreign investment.

Some individuals in China have become very rich. One should not, however, confuse the ability of a few to acquire private wealth with economic development. The political economy of Third World nations makes it easier for the well-connected to enrich themselves than does a free market system. This explains why, in many poor, developing countries, the current or former ruling families and their cronies are (or were) so rich (e.g., the Salinas, the Suhartos, Adnan Kasogi in his heyday, the late Ferdinand Marcos). To be successful in business in China one needs a "roof," that is, someone in authority who sells protection. One's fortunes rise and fall with those of the protector, rather than according to the laws of supply and demand. And, if the "roof" shields the businessman from competition, both can enjoy the economic rent of monopolies or oligopolies, which enriches them and impoverishes the country.

In addition, one should also be wary of accepting Chinese statistics at face value. Measuring the economy of a nation of over a billion people while it undergoes a major transition is an art, not an exact science. In addition, the inability of the government to raise taxes effectively indicates that it has no grasp over the economy.[33] Moreover, communist authorities show scant regard for the truth. Paul Krugman noted, at the end of 1994, that "Chinese statistics on foreign investment have been overstated by as much as a factor of 6."[34] Thus, while Chinese exports indicate that the Chinese economy has been expanding, one should be careful about exaggerated claims of economic success.

Related to economic issues, China's environmental damage will slow future growth. The true extent of the ecological crisis is still unclear; but if recent articles and the Soviet experience are any guide, ecological problems will probably slow Chinese progress more than it has in other Asian states. The mismanagement of agriculture may hinder food production; foreign pressure could derail industrial projects, and pollution could have costly side effects, such as brain damage and premature deaths of working-age Chinese.

In fact, China currently faces many obstacles to further economic development. The most important of these is the absence of an effective legal and institutional framework. A developed economy requires sophisticated and reliable property laws, courts, tax authorities, and police forces. Once a country reaches a certain stage of development, it must either have created these legal institutions or remain mired in limbo, with pockets of development of varying size coexisting with a large, inefficient, and low-productivity sector.

The lack of institutional development in China explains why, for example, the biggest inroads against poverty date from the early 1980s, just after the liberalization of farming; and why progress since has slowed down.[35] The People's Republic has few of the institutions essential to a developed economy. Therefore, it is likely to fail in its quest to emulate South Korea or Taiwan.

The first roadblock to Chinese development is that businesses cannot rely on laws, because the nation either has no laws to address commercial issues or does not implement them well. Property rights are ill-formed at best; and even where laws exist, the courts and police forces are neither properly trained nor willing to uphold them. Judges obey the party's orders and are more likely to have studied Marxism than law.

In particular, there is an absence of a clear and effective real estate law. It is possible for private individuals to lease land—at this point private individuals and "feudal entities" (army, state-related organizations, government-owned corporations, etc.) control the use of land—but no one has a clear title to it.[36] Investors may buy a house but not the land on which it sits.[37] A survey found that many farmers do not know the duration of their land rights.[38] This situation slows the creation of a bourgeoisie because a middle class without real property ownership is a contradiction in terms. It also hinders investment and increases the unpredictability of doing business in China. Unfortunately for China, this problem will be difficult to solve. Abolishing the landlord class was a pillar of the communist revolution. To accept a return to unrestricted private land ownership goes against the grain of the communist ethos and would mobilize ideological and economic foes of reform. Even in Russia, which has formally renounced communism, there has been no effective introduction of unrestrained private land ownership in agriculture.

The second roadblock to development is that, as a result of the legal void just described, China is highly corrupt. Transparency International ranked the PRC 41 (out of 52) in its yearly corruption rankings (the No. 1 slot being for the least corrupt nation), far below the other Sinic societies of Taiwan, Hong Kong, and Singapore.[39] Corruption is endemic in the country. Dignitaries and military officers participate in shady deals, and local officials routinely profit from crime.[40] Mayfair Mei-hui Yang discovered a "society of gatekeepers" and "tolltakers,"[41] in which countless officials demand bribes from citizens. Freedom House noted in May 1996, that "corruption and connections are the keys to entrepreneurial success" in a system that has "enriched a corrupt network of ruling elites." Freedom House concluded that China had a very low level of economic freedom (2/16 versus 11 for Taiwan and 12 for Singapore), a view shared by the 1997 *Index of Economic Freedom.*[42]

Optimists argue that corruption in the PRC should not be judged according to Western norms, especially America's Puritan ones. They claim that what Americans call corruption is a respectable and effective standard operating procedure in Asia. This is false. Kickbacks and bribes which subvert market forces are as damaging to national prosperity in Asia as in the West. Rich Asian countries, such as Singapore and Japan, are, by the West's own standards, no more corrupt than comparable Western nations; and the poorest West European regions, e.g., southern Italy and Greece, are highly corrupt. The complex causality between poverty and corruption is beyond the scope of this study, but it is clear is that China's corruption is both a source and a symptom of its problems, and a major obstacle to economic growth.

Finally, the PRC lacks an effective tax system. A communist government owns everything and does not need to tax the (officially nonexistent) private sector. The planning system, rather than the market and tax-financed government spending, allocates all resources throughout the economy. A capitalist state, however, must tax. Raising revenue is most challenging because it involves taking money from people who will do their best to avoid paying. As communism's grip on the economy weakens, the regime will soon have to find a way to finance itself effectively. So far, it has failed in its endeavor. The absence of a working tax system is a huge obstacle to further progress; its magnitude cannot be overstated.[43]

China-boosters say that China will soon change. They note that unfair law enforcement was a hallmark of South Korea and Taiwan for many decades. The PRC, however, is not the Taiwan or South Korea of thirty years ago. In the 1960s, South Korea and Taiwan already possessed the basic institutions of capitalism—i.e., property rights, business law, and law courts. Implementation was spotty, and sometimes unfair, but the state was an entity within which the institutions of capitalism either already existed or from which they could emerge.

The Chinese state today, however, is not one in which capitalism can grow steadily. Institutional systems are generally so embedded in the structure and psychology of a society that they cannot change rapidly. Moreover, there are high transaction costs associated with erecting new institutions.[44] For example, the transaction cost of altering property rights (slavery) in the American South was a civil war. Likewise, to a Chinese tolltaker a less corrupt society would be catastrophic. His income would plummet, and he would have to get a real job. Finally, because many of those who are corrupt are very powerful, deposing them would entail a full-scale revolution.

Improving institutions requires more than legislation. Many states have enacted good laws; few have been successful in putting them into practice. This is because even as laws are modified, the weight of history and the "imbeddedness of informal constraints in societies" slow down progress. Mindsets do not change rapidly.[45] England enjoys the rule of law today because the roots of law in that nation go back centuries. As early as the 1590s we can hear, in Shakespeare's *Richard III,* the Duke of Clarence crying out to the murderers in the pay of his evil sibling, "before I be convict by course of law, /To threaten me with death is most unlawful." Respect for the rule of law takes generations to become part of a society's consciousness.

The Chinese path diverged from that of Taiwan and Korea at least a century ago, when Japan colonized them. China cannot simply copy their institutions and policies. Societies evolve in response to new environments, but their future shape is restricted by their past conditions. Development is "path-dependent:" past choices determine the options available in the future, and China's status as a nation on the "wrong road" restricts its ability to move to the right one, as the following discussion indicates. In other words, "history matters."

The rule of law and private property are anathema to communists, and China—unlike Taiwan, South Korea, and Japan—underwent decades of communism. Even today, though communism in China has acquired many "Chinese characteristics," the Communist party is still in charge at the top. It controls the bureaucracy as part of its nomenklatura. There is none of the autonomous and qualified civil service structure which allowed Japan, Korea, and Taiwan to compensate for their weak legal framework.[46] The Chinese civil service consists of party loyalists rather than men selected through rigorous exams, as is the case in a country like South Korea.

Moreover, some former communist subjects, such as the Czechs, enjoyed the rule of law and prosperity prior to the imposition of communism. Fragments of their old bourgeois political and legal culture survived the Marxist-Leninist tyranny. China's people, however, have never experienced the rule of law. The communist era was preceded by decades of fighting and unrest.

Nor does China's imperial past contain a legal tradition which could assist a capitalist transformation. As William C. Jones has explained in *The Great Qing Code,*[47] traditional Chinese law concerned itself with issues involving officials or the state's interests (such as taxes or social order). It did not regulate suits affecting individuals in need of arbitrators in which the state had no stake (e.g., torts, contracts). The Code was a manual for government administrators rather than a legal statute in the Roman or Napoleonic sense: "Civil law as the law which deals with the private concerns of citizens from the point of view of those citizens did not exist in the [Qing] Code."[48] And China does not have the common law tradition which England and its former colonies have used effectively as a substitute for code law.

As for communism, it also has no legal tradition of any use in the development of a market economy. There is no private sector in communist societies and thus no need to legislate a framework for it. In any event, because the party is above the law, the concept of the rule of law as understood in the West is alien to Marxist-Leninists.

Beyond rules and regulations, a nation's strength and stability are underpinned by its civil society—the clubs, independent churches, and economic associations that lie between the purview of the state and the realm of the family. Civil society is difficult to quantify, but it is extremely important in fostering development, as Robert Putnam's *Making Democracy Work* demonstrates.[49] Some have argued persuasively that some forms of civil society may hinder political development (see *Hudson Institute's Briefing Paper* No. 196, by John Clark).[50] Nevertheless, some sort of civil society is needed for a country to prosper. Chinese society is highly deficient in this area. Groups and organizations free of state control have always been disliked by the communist regime and its predecessors. As a result, the people's lack of experience with "[t]he fundamental nature of social obligations has been a major obstacle to China developing a sense of citizenship."[51] Though wealthy individuals and businesses now give to charities, they do so to pay off the authorities by financing welfare schemes in exchange for their support. Because of the decaying nature of communist rule, criminal-like associations and other cliques which a faithless and venal regime is wont to produce might be the major elements of China's future civil society. In many post-communist societies, the most vital "civil society" associations have been these corrupt communist networks and their related "mafias" which hinder rather than foster liberal economic and political development.

China also lacks a strong, property-owning bourgeoisie. This class is essential to a nation's ability to uphold property rights and the rule of law, at least in the economic sphere, because while the middle classes everywhere may be happy to have political dissidents jailed, they also want a reliable system of contract enforcement. To the extent that there is a business class in China, it is "markedly apolitical" and has not created a bourgeois civil society.[52] The Chinese bourgeoisie's atrophied state is the outcome of communist rule, and remains an obstacle to stable economic growth.

Finally, as Richard Pipes noted in *Commentary,* modernization is Westernization.[53] There are only two categories of rich non-Western countries. The first consists of underpopulated oil monarchies, which are weak polities without national cohesion. Their wealth (or rather that of the owning families) is an accident of geology.

The second group of rich non-Western nations is made up of the countries of East Asia. All of these countries have undergone extensive and lengthy Westernization. Japan, for example, imported many Western institutions in the Meiji era and lived for six years under the proconsulate of an American general, Douglas MacArthur. Japanese ministries and companies still send many young professionals to American and European universities, and, with apt symbolism, the next imperial couple will be Oxford- and Harvard-educated. Japan's culture is Japanese, rooted in Japan's tradition and the great Chinese contribution.[54] The importation of Western institutions does not indicate the end to the cultural essence of Japanness. The relevant fact, however, is that Japan's economic, legal, and political system is far more Western than "Asian," and has been so for over a century. (Readers must not equate Western with American. Japanese politics and legal norms from the late nineteenth century to the present have been very different from American ones but are quite similar to those found in countries like Germany, France, and Italy).

South Korea and Taiwan, the other notable non-Western success stories of the century, went through two stages of Westernization. First, Japan imposed Japanese-mediated Western institutions on them. The Japanese occupation of Korea is remembered for its harshness, culminating in the atrocities of the "comfort women" and the humiliating policy of forcing Koreans to adopt Japanese names. Nevertheless, the Japanese period is of great importance in understanding contemporary Korea and Taiwan.[55] First, the Japanese regime "swept away the indigenous ruling institutions and elite in Taiwan and Korea."[56] Then, Japanese administrators laid in each the foundations of an industrial society. They undertook comprehensive land surveys, and instituted systematic property taxes. They also modernized the health and education systems and, in Taiwan, installed an effective police force. Native subjects manned the colonial bureaucracies except for the top echelons, providing experience in the functioning of modern administrative organizations. The late president Park Chung-Hee of South Korea, the father of industrialization, graduated from a Japanese military academy (in Manchukuo). President Lee Teng-hui of the ROC has a degree from Kyoto University and speaks better Japanese than Mandarin Chinese. Of course, Korea did not have to endure Japanese colonialism. A modernizing Yi dynasty, which had started to seek western technology and American support in the late nineteenth century, could have modernized Korea without the pain and humiliation of conquest. The fact remains, however, that South Korea and Taiwan today are products of a Westernization process that started a century ago.

After World War II, the American military, U.S. advisers, and the education of the elite in American colleges and universities further implanted Western methods in Korea and Taiwan. Migration to North America also increased cultural ties between Koreans and Taiwanese and the West. Finally, Protestantism and Roman Catholicism, which foster Western ideals and brings ties with Christians in America and Europe, has developed rapidly in South Korea, and to a lesser extent in Taiwan.

The potential for significant Western or Japanese influence in China is poor. The West's ability to influence China is minimal. The U.S. Army will not occupy China, nor will Britain or Japan colonize it. China's 1.24 billion people dilute the impact of returning students and visiting businessmen. (In order to duplicate Taiwan's ratio of students who receive higher education in the U.S. and its percentage of citizens who travel abroad, China would have to send 2.1 million students to America and 350,000 to Japan [over eighteen times the current number for the U.S.] and 230 million tourists from the mainland would have to leave the country every year.) There are hundreds of millions of Chinese peasants in the hinterland, cut off from cosmopolitan maritime winds. Even in a relatively small Taiwan, Westernization and modernization took a long time; in a nation the size of China, the time frame would need to be much longer, unless incredible improvements in education and applied psychology take place very quickly.

Some observers have written that the PRC is following the *fukoku kyohei* (i.e, rich country, strong army) track of Meiji Japan.[57] The Meiji reformers, however, threw out much of Japan's political and legal practices and imported Western law and organization. Their decisions were made easier by the fact that they had no choice. Europeans and Americans had extraterritorial rights which threatened to make Japan a vassal of the Western nations. The Westerners demanded that Japan adopt Western legal practices before they surrendered their extraterritorial privileges.

Japan's Meiji rulers erected the revitalized imperial throne as a symbol of eternal Japan to mask the revolutionary extent of change which they themselves probably did not fully understand in 1868. By the turn of the century, the political and economic life of Japan had more in common with William II's Germany than with old Japan. China's current leaders, on the other hand, "commit the government to the nineteenth century fallacy that China could join the modern world on its own terms."[58] The PRC government seeks to avoid the consequences of Westernization. Its policies resemble the "wealth and strength" reforms of the Qing dynasty following its defeat at the hands of England and France in 1860, when China sought to adapt Western technology without "socio-political reconstruction."[59]

Some Chinese hope to apply the "Hong Kong model" or the "Singapore model" to China.[60] They see the Chinese city-states as a perfect mix of capitalist wealth and "Chinese" order. They prefer Singapore to the undisciplined democracy of Taiwan, where the KMT's monopoly on power has been dented. The "politics-free" environment of Hong Kong prior to Governor Patton's reforms of Singapore, they believe, can be transplanted to China. This concept is, superficially, plausible because Hong Kong and Singapore are prosperous Chinese societies.

China, however, cannot replicate the city states' experiences. First, there are four hundred times more people in China than on Singapore and two hundred times more than in Hong Kong. The political situations are totally different. In Hong Kong, the British colonial administration froze political life in a way that only an alien but impartial government could. In Singapore, the fear of ethnic Chinese surrounded by Sinophobes in Malaysia and Indonesia provided a remarkable level of national cohesion and purpose. Moreover, with a long experience of British administration, and thus the rule of law, Singapore and Hong Kong diverged from China over a century ago. As immigrant urban societies they are distinct from China, where hundreds of millions of peasants farm their ancestral land. More importantly, the infatuation for Singapore or Hong Kong on the part of Beijing autocrats shows a lack of understanding of what makes these cities rich. Singapore is not as democratic or free as the United States. However, it is a state where the rule of law (at least for commercial transactions), a qualified civil service, freedom of movement, and strong property rights are the norm (Freedom House ranks it as partly free, on a par with Turkey; it considers China not free, giving the country its lowest ranking).[61] The political economy of Singapore resembles that of Switzerland more than it does China's. "Singapore Inc." is light-years from the shady deals and undefined property rights of the PRC. As for Hong Kong, its prosperity is based on the rule of law; it owes its freedom to the mother of modern capitalism and the land of the *Magna Carta.* President Jiang Zemin declared that Hong Kong's prosperity results mainly from the creativity of the Hong Kong people themselves, and cannot be attributed to an independent judiciary and a free press.[62] While no one underestimates Hong Kongers' dynamism, this statement demonstrates a failure to understand economic development. All countries have bright people; but only a few, like Hong Kong, have the institutions which allow entrepreneurs to thrive and enrich their nation at the same time.

In addition, the international environment is a greater burden for China than it has been for Japan, Taiwan, and South Korea since 1945. South Korea and Taiwan devoted significant resources to their militaries, but barring a communist onslaught, their strategic environment was rather benign. The United States maintained regional security; and, except for some maritime disputes, they did not need to worry about border problems (Taiwan and Japan are islands and South Korea has no other land border besides the DMZ). China, on the other hand, borders fourteen states on land, not including the Special Administrative Region of Hong Kong and Macao. It shares contiguous territorial waters with Taiwan's offshore islands, and has overlapping maritime claims against several other nations. Furthermore, several Asian countries have large ethnic Chinese communities whose members have real or perceived ties to the mainland. Thus, China is bound to be involved in disputes and conflicts with some of its neighbors. Its sheer mass makes it difficult for China to avoid foreign entanglements. Unlike Japan or Korea, it cannot, for various reasons, enjoy the benefits of the U.S. strategic umbrella. Consequently, international disputes are more likely to disturb Chinese economic progress than they did that of Japan, South Korea, Taiwan, or Singapore.

RELATIVE POWER COMPARED TO JAPAN

If the United States disengages from East Asia, China and Japan will confront each other. Military power, even if not used in battle, will play an important role in deciding the correlation of power between China and Japan. Because Japan is so superior to China in economic power, military might provides Beijing its only hope for raising its status vis-à-vis Japan. Unfortunately for China, Japan will emerge as the stronger power in any arms race, thus depriving China of any hopes of regional military supremacy in the wake of a U.S.

withdrawal. To understand why Japan, and not China is Asia's potential superpower, one must review some economic and industrial facts.

Japan has a $4.8 trillion economy; China's is probably less than $1 trillion.[63] (It is difficult to quantify China's economy but the order of magnitude is clear.) The qualitative gap between Japan's technologically advanced society and China is even greater (a good benchmark is Japan's $38,000 of per capita income compared to China's $720). Some scholars magnify China's economy by resorting to purchasing power parities (PPPs) which take into account the lower prices in China compared to those in Japan. PPPs compare standards of living across borders but cannot measure national power. Admittedly, some defense costs are linked to wage levels. A billion dollars pays for more soldier man-hours in China than in Japan (but the education of the average Japanese is superior, making him better prepared and easier to train). Overall, PPPs do not reflect military power potential; they can merely compensate for exchange rate abnormalities and differences in prices for domestic goods and services, such as land and wages. Imported military goods or fuel, for example, have a world price that is unaffected by PPP. Buying foreign technology is not cheaper for China than for Japan. Moreover, the production and maintenance of advanced weapons are less expensive in rich countries than in poor ones because the latter's low cost of labor and land does not compensate for unreliable transportation and communication networks, and an uneven technological base. In poor nations, low wages do not balance the costs of abysmal productivity and reliability.

Furthermore, power requires money. For example, one reason for the successes of the U.S.-sponsored Middle East peace process from 1973 onward is America's ability to write big checks to its allies. Financial resources make it possible to exert influence over international institutions (e.g., the World Trade Organization, the International Monetary Fund, and development banks), and thus affect other nations' military power by affecting their economies. This capability is measured at current exchange rates, not on the basis of PPP. Rich countries can also block their companies from investing in countries they oppose, as the United States has done with Iran and Cuba. They can even influence the behavior of other countries' corporations. Poorer nations like China, regardless of their PPP income, have far less influence because they are not home to large corporations and have less influence on international investors.

Japan has a middle-sized military, the Self-Defense Forces (SDF). This military is considered superior to China's PLA in areas such as air power, and in the command-and-control systems that are so important in war. Nevertheless, neither Japan nor China is a military superpower. But this is so because China cannot afford to be one, whereas Japan could become a superpower if it wanted, as the following discussion explains.

With 125 million inhabitants, Japan can raise a large military. Its population is aging, but military power also relies on noncombatants (engineers, technicians, intelligence analysts, etc.) who need not be young men. The Japanese are extremely well educated. The high level of scientific education and literacy among the lower and lower-middle classes provides the SDF with one of the world's best-trained manpower pools for enlisted personnel. Japan's wealth could allow it to spend almost $300 billion a year on defense without bankrupting the country's treasury. (An armament program could go as far as trebling defense spending. This would still leave Japan spending well under 5 percent of GDP on defense, current spending being in the 1 to 1.4 percent range depending on accounting methods (the higher figure is mostly the result of including the cost of Imperial armed forces veterans). If defense spending rose, however, these outlays would be unaffected).[64] A more ambitious program, devoting say ¥34 trillion to the SDF (US$285 billion), up from a planned ¥5-7 trillion for 1997,[65] would only equal 7 percent of GDP. This percentage is barely more than what the U.S. appropriated for the Pentagon in 1985, and similar to the 1985 defense efforts of Taiwan and Singapore. Because Japan's economy is huge, this sum equals the entire GDP of Taiwan or Switzerland.[66]

Moreover, Japan's technological base is outstanding. The human and technological capital in firms such as Toshiba, Nikkei, Fujitsu, Mitsui, and Matsushita cannot be replicated rapidly. Few nations have such national assets, and China is certainly not one of them. Japan does not have a large military-industrial complex, but its industries' advances in automation, miniaturization, robotics, optronics, and other areas give it "latent military-industrial capabilities."[67] About $138 billion is spent annually on research and development in Japan.[68] Along with these resources, the international network of Japanese businesses and the experience gained by the Japanese who work abroad could be conjoined to lay the foundations of a sophisticated human intelligence agency. Also, although Japan is densely populated, it does have areas with few inhabitants. Moreover, because of its wealth, Japan could lease land overseas to train its soldiers and pilots in combined large-scale arms operations and long-range deployment.

Also important is Japan's alliance with the United States. Because of its extensive business ties to North America and Europe, Japan can readily establish joint weapons programs with other advanced countries. (Indeed, U.S. and Japanese industry already cooperate on some armaments programs.) Japanese money and achievements in militarily-relevant areas such as ceramics, robotics, and flat computer screens, give Tokyo bargaining power in technology transfers, whereas China can offer nothing of the sort. Japan's deep pockets allow it to make financial contributions in lieu of technology if needed.

China's military power, by contrast, is quite limited. The PRC, larger than the U.S., with over 1.2 billion inhabitants and more than two million soldiers, is almost invasion-proof. Except by resorting to genocide, no foreign invader could control China's population; nor is it conceivable that an invader would have an interest in contemplating such action. A large population alone, however, does not make a country a superpower or allow it to project much power internationally, as India and its 975 million inhabitants demonstrate. China's offensive power is limited by several factors, as the brief analysis shows:

Maintaining internal order is the primary task of the People's Liberation Army. Because of its role in keeping the Communist party in power, the PLA cannot focus on preparing to fight other armies. This situation cannot easily be remedied because to do so would diminish the regime's ability to counter real and imagined domestic foes. In addition, economic constraints prevent the PLA from building up a large, first-rate military. Because of poor relations with the United States and a need to save money, China has bought Russian equipment, and most Russian weapons are inferior to Western ones and difficult to maintain. Moreover, Russia's reliability as a supplier of spare parts is doubtful because of its political and economic instability.

The Chinese military contains elite units that are well-trained and highly motivated, and there are "pockets of excellence" within the PLA. But although these forces might win local conflicts, such as a border war with Vietnam or India, they cannot evict the U.S. military from Asia or invade Japan or South Korea. The PLA lacks the heavy firepower and logistics to compete with the U.S. Army, and the Chinese air and naval forces are no match for their American counterparts. The U.S. infrastructure in airlift, command and control, electronic warfare and intelligence, and space-based systems far surpasses anything China can hope to field. Neither can China duplicate the investments in education and training the U.S. armed forces have undertaken. The insistence on a high degree of self-sufficiency in defense acquisition has also hindered China's military modernization.[69] Japan, on the other hand, has the resources to build a modern military apparatus which would rapidly surpass China's because of its industrial and technological assets and its far more effective state apparatus.

One can argue that technology and wealth are not enough and that China can compensate for its technological inferiority. There are examples of "low-technology" forces that have defeated modern armies. Consider, for example, the Zulus' victories against the British and the Vietnamese communists' against France and the United States.[70] In all these cases, however, the "low technology" side had the advantage of operating at home against foreigners. Moreover, the end result was that the British defeated the Zulus, and the Vietnamese enjoyed considerable foreign assistance from China and the Soviet Union.

For power projection, a country with fewer economic and technological resources is at a massive disadvantage. Mao emphasized the ability of motivated soldiers to defeat superior forces, but at some point this "military romanticism" cannot overcome sheer firepower. For example, in spite of great courage, ideological and patriotic fervor, and blunders on the part of the Americans, the PLA's 1950-51 campaign in Korea failed because the firepower and logistics of the Americans were so superior to China's.[71] (Likewise, at Nomonhan in 1939, Soviet armor defeated Japanese military romanticism). Although a future "revolution in military affairs" (RMA) could break the linkage between economic strength and military might, the correlation between the two will remain valid for the foreseeable future. Some experts think that, by implementing an information-warfare type of RMA, China might become a great military power. But even these experts admit that this would require shifting PLA doctrine toward individualism, which goes against the grain of the regime.[72] Besides, even if such an RMA could be implemented, either by the PRC or a post-communist government, it is difficult to see how its impact could materialize in less than a couple of decades.

Technologically backward countries, moreover, have generally compensated for their lack in this area by a combination of superior political organization and motivation. The Chinese communists during the civil war provide a good example of such a situation. The PRC, today, does not have this advantage. Japan, not China, is politically and internally stronger. Japan is a stable democracy. Its constitutional order has functioned well for almost half a century, and the country has a solid middle class. Unlike China, Japan has been united and safe from breakup for more than 350 years. It is far less likely to be rocked by revolution or power struggles than China. Today's Japanese state is much stronger than the Chinese one. The capacity of Japan to mobilize resources in pursuit of a national goal is far greater than that of the PRC, whose regime lacks the administrative effectiveness of a modern state.

China does have some advantages. Against Taiwan, for example, China can utilize psychological warfare and subversion. Through its demographic weight and cultural ties, and the disunity of ASEAN (the Association of Southeast Asian Nations), China has cast a long shadow over Southeast Asia. As James Shinn wrote in *Weaving the Net,* overseas Chinese business people "may well be exploited by Beijing to exert subtle but effective pressure on ASEAN governments,"[73] and the ability of the PRC to help the Khmer Rouge against the Vietnamese showed "many intimate and well-placed covert contacts in the Chinese community in Bangkok."[74] China can also intimidate weaker neighbors in Central Asia, and might even be able to threaten the Russian Far East if the Russian Federation declines in strength.

Thus, an indirect strategy might work in Southeast Asia and Taiwan, and China's great size might allow it to dominate weaker neighbors. China's direct and indirect power, however, will remain ineffective against Japan and the United States, and these nations are the key to regional stability. The Japanese and U.S. economies are so large that China's looks far less impressive from Tokyo or Washington than from Singapore or Bangkok. Also, although China can exploit the ethnic Chinese in Southeast Asia because many suffer from discrimination, this leverage will not work in Japan (or Korea) because there is no significant ethnic Chinese population; it will also fail in America, where Chinese-Americans are free from the institutionalized discrimination common to several Southeast Asian states. In Northeast Asia, China might try to manipulate Korean resentment against Japan (and the U.S.) to bring a unified Korea into its own sphere of influence. However, effective diplomacy by the United States, which is better able to provide Korea with security and markets than China, can preempt such a stratagem. Even in Taiwan, a credible American commitment can compensate for China's special position.

Consequently, if the result of Korean unification is Sino-Japanese confrontation, China will likely emerge not only as the economically weaker party but also the militarily weaker one. The benign, though irritating, *pax americana* may be replaced, then, by a dangerous rivalry between a strong and modern Japan, and an unstable and weak China.

CONCLUSION

Although it is impossible to predict the future of China, many clouds glower on the horizon. It is no accident that many well-connected Chinese from the PRC invest their profits overseas rather than plow them back into Chinese ventures.[75] Economic and political expectations are growing faster than they can be met. And, unfortunately for the regime, the working class has been raised on a diet of Marxist ideology, which facilitates its mobilization only in revolutionary enterprises.

China's situation has almost nothing in common with those of the smaller East Asian nations. The turmoil of post-communist states, especially those that lack a tradition of the rule of law and could not rely on proximity to the West, may be a better indicator of China's future than the growth and relative stability of Taiwan and Korea. Neither a communist nor a capitalist China may remain for decades in the limbo of "an administered market to emerge that allows the gatekeepers extravagant rents."[76]

Consequently, China is ill-equipped to face the challenges which will confront it after Korean unification. Its government officials' public self-confidence hides a fragile polity with limited resources. Turmoil in post-unification Asia could be extremely dangerous for Beijing's rulers.

Moonbae-do (*Haetae*-mythical lion) designates pictures which people used to put, at the beginning of the year, on the gates and doors to wish happiness and protect the house from bad things. Four kinds of animals—Tiger, *Haetae* or mythical lion, Chicken, Dog—were usually painted, and each of them had a particular placement according to its symbolic meaning. Art courtesy of MINHWA-Korean Folk Art Prints © 1994 Editions API, Seoul, Korea.

CHAPTER FIVE
RUSSIA

Although Russia's importance on the Korean peninsula has arguably dwindled since the collapse of the Soviet Union, it would be foolish to disregard Russia completely in a survey of security in Northeast Asia. Certainly Russia's internal problems have weakened her leverage in the region, but she does not plan to remain on the periphery forever. As this chapter will argue, it is precisely this weakness that drives Russia to seek attention in the region. More than anything else, Russia wants to be included in security arrangements in Northeast Asia—particularly those on the Korean peninsula. For this reason, Russia has great potential either to stabilize or seriously undermine peace in Northeast Asia.

Russia's policy in Northeast Asia in general—and on the Korean peninsula in particular—has vacillated significantly since the collapse of the Soviet Union. This vacillation was born from competing foreign policy visions in Russia's internal politics. As this chapter will argue, different Asian neighbors gained diplomatic ground as Russia implemented contrasting visions. Policy with Japan has come full circle since Russia's independence, and there have also been swings in the foreign policy pendulum on the Korean peninsula. These policy fluctuations have so far cost Russia its primary objective—becoming a major actor in Asia.

This chapter is divided into eight sections and a conclusion. The first section reviews Soviet foreign policy in the Asian Pacific Region prior to the collapse of the Soviet Union. The second section outlines the West-centric foreign policy which Russia initially adopted after independence; the third explains the change toward a more Eurasianist perspective. This led to a renewed focus on better relations with China (the subject of the fourth section), although this Sino-centric policy was opposed in the Russian Far East—as the fifth section outlines. The chapter then turns to the Korean peninsula, as sections six and seven describe the conflicting half-measures which Russia adopted toward the ROK and DPRK. These inconsistent policies marginalized Russia in international negotiations about issues on the peninsula. The eighth section outlines Russia's three-pronged approach for dealing with this diplomatic isolation.

Soviet Foreign Policy in Northeast Asia

Before its collapse, the Soviet Union was militarily, though not economically, a part of the Asia Pacific region. This unidimensional policy developed from two events in Northeast Asia: first, the division of the Korean peninsula in 1945 which was finalized by the 1953 armistice and subsequent partition of Northeast Asia into "two camps;" and second, the Sino-Soviet split in 1957. As a result, with the exception of North Korea, the Soviet Union maintained tense relations with most of its Asian neighbors. In the case of Japan and the Republic of Korea, both were viewed as U.S. satellites and thus targets of Soviet hostility. In the case of China, the Soviet decision not to finance Chinese industrialization laid the foundations for the Sino-Soviet split and spurred two decades of arms buildup along their lengthy common border. Thus, the Soviet Union's only ally in Northeast Asia was the Democratic People's Republic of Korea (DPRK). As an extension of the Sino-Soviet competition, the Soviet Union signed a Treaty of Mutual Friendship and Support with Pyongyang in 1961, and provided it with subsidized oil and other goods on a concessionary basis. North Korea used its position to play the PRC and the Soviet Union against each other, but Moscow eventually gained the upper hand in the 1980's through its assistance in building the DPRK's military.[1]

By the mid-1980s this unidimensional and ruinously expensive military policy had begun to lose its effectiveness, setting the stage for a profound revolution in Soviet foreign policy under Mikhail Gorbachev. During the six years he was in power, Gorbachev fundamentally revised the three central tenets of postwar Soviet policy in East Asia—he ended the ineffective and costly Sino-Soviet conflict; he suppressed the dominant bipolar East-West antagonism and thus shifted Soviet policy towards Japan and the Republic of Korea; and finally, he began a demilitarizing policy that opened the possibility of economic relations with East Asian states.[2] Gorbachev first articulated this new strategy for the Asia Pacific region in his July 1986 Vladivostok speech, in which he outlined five new policy thrusts: (i) he said the Soviet Union would seek bilateral relations with all states in the region, including China and the Republic of Korea; (ii) he voiced support for nuclear nonproliferation in the Asia Pacific region; (iii) he argued for creating limits in naval forces in the region; (iv) he called for reductions in the force buildup along the Sino-Soviet border; (v) he argued that the region needed a multilateral forum that would help to establish confidence building measures between states in the region.[3]

This new policy vision was quickly reinforced when Gorbachev addressed China's "three obstacles" to better Sino-Soviet relations: Vietnamese troop withdrawal from Cambodia, Soviet retreat from Mongolia and Afghanistan, and a reduction in the Soviet forces massed along China's northern border. Between 1987 and his arrival in Beijing for the May 1989 summit, Gorbachev made unilateral concessions on all three issues and cleared the way for a Sino-Soviet rapprochement.[4] A similar rapprochement occurred with the Republic of Korea after the June 1990 San Francisco meeting between Gorbachev and President Roh Tae-Woo. The two countries established diplomatic ties four months later, and the ROK rewarded Gorbachev's overtures with a $3 billion loan in 1991.[5]

With the Vladivostok speech, Gorbachev discarded the old Soviet military stability in the region in the hope of creating a new stability, in which the Soviet Union would be a major inside actor. Gorbachev imagined that, as an inside actor, the Soviet Union would benefit both economically and politically. Unfortunately for Gorbachev, the new policy met with qualified success. Despite improvements in relations with China and South Korea, the unresolved Northern Territories (or Southern Kurile Islands) issue and a continuing trade deficit hindered Soviet-Japanese relations. In addition, the collapsing economy made it less and less possible for the Soviet Union to continue funding the DPRK's weapons buildup. We can only speculate whether Gorbachev's policy would have been more successful in the long term because it was at this moment that his mandate ran out. The collapse of the Soviet Union effectively ended Gorbachev's policy in Northeast Asia.

RUSSIA'S WEST-CENTRIC FOREIGN POLICY

Following his ascent to power late in 1991, Boris Yeltsin promoted proponents of radical economic reform in domestic politics and of internationalist perspectives in foreign policy to top leadership positions, and independent Russia initially adopted their foreign policy course. The central argument of this liberal group was that Russia's foreign policy priority should be to join the "civilized" (Western) world. As Foreign Minister Andrei Kozyrev said in January 1992, "The developed countries of the West are Russia's natural allies."[6] This group's initial goals were to establish a strategic alliance with the United States, to ensure financial assistance from the West, and to integrate Russia into international economic and political institutions. Variously called the "internationalists" or "Atlanticists," the main proponents of this perspective were Kozyrev, the economists of the first government (Yegor Gaidar and Gennady Burbulis), and Yeltsin himself.[7]

This West-centric policy orientation had two implications for Russian policy in Northeast Asia. First, it discouraged close relations with the DPRK and China and argued for letting the Near Abroad states in Central Asia fend for themselves. Second, it meant aligning Russia with the Western security system in Northeast Asia. Russia had two paths through which it could enter this U.S.-based security system: either direct negotiation with Washington or indirect engagement through close cooperation with one or more of its Asian partners. Russia embarked on the second path, through improved relations with Japan and the ROK.[8]

In the case of Japan, the Russian leaders knew they needed to resolve the dispute over the Northern Territories (Southern Kuriles), which lie off the coast of northern Japan and had been seized by the Soviet Army in the final days of World War II. Japan's insistence that the islands be returned to Japan had precluded the signing of a peace treaty, and the unwillingness of nationalists in both countries to compromise on the issue has constituted the principal stumbling block to friendly relations between Moscow and Tokyo ever since.[9] In August 1991, however, the Russian Atlanticists seemed to be moving toward a breakthrough on the issue. In a visit to Japan two weeks after the aborted coup, Ruslan Khasbulatov stressed that the issue must be dealt with in a way that respected international "law and justice." The Russian government reinstalled the validity of the 1956 Joint Declaration and offered to return Shitokan and the Habomai, two of the islands (the two smallest ones; Hatomai itself being a cluster of small islands), on the conclusion of a peace treaty.[10] Yeltsin apparently hoped that by offering territorial concessions he would encourage greater Japanese involvement in Russia's economic transformation. This conciliatory policy continued through early August 1992, when Deputy Prime Minister Mikhail Poltaranin in Tokyo reaffirmed Russian willingness to give up the two islands and negotiate the future status of Kunashiri and Etorofu (the two bigger islands).[11]

Despite this promising start, relations between Japan and Russia soon stalled. Japan insisted on the return of all four islands, and by Autumn 1992, sentiment in Russia had changed. Retaining the Southern Kurile Islands is one of several litmus tests by which the willingness of politicians to stand up for Russia's "nationalist interests" has been judged. Thus, domestic opposition to territorial concessions ended the conciliatory policy toward Japan, even causing Yeltsin abruptly to cancel a planned visit. The Atlanticist viewpoint had lasted only six months; Russian domestic politics had begun to shift toward the "Eurasianist" perspective.

RUSSIA'S EURASIANIST FOREIGN POLICY

Disenchantment with the West began when the expected Japanese and Western aid did not materialize; it was, moreover, strengthened by frustration over the difficulties of integrating into world economic and diplomatic institutions. Russia was not admitted into the Asia-Pacific Economic Cooperation (APEC) forum, and it waited fruitlessly for improved trading rights with the European Union.[12] Finally, Russian attempts at mediation in the former Yugoslavia, and disagreement over the possible expansion of NATO, met with Western resistance on several occasions. All of these events helped to trigger a swing in domestic opinion concerning foreign policy. The shift was made evident by Yeltsin's remarks in January 1993 during a visit to India: "We need to maintain," he said, "a balance in our foreign policy relations with the West and the East." His visits to South Korea, India, and China were, in his view, "indicative of the fact that we are moving away from a Western emphasis."[13]

Domestic criticism of the Atlanticist perspective originated in the Parliament, but also encompassed a broad segment of the intelligentsia. Their critique centered on five issues. First, they argued, the Atlanticists had unrealistic expectations about Western support, which had not been not borne out in foreign aid and assistance. Second, the Atlanticist policies failed to identify and protect Russia's national interests, as well as to perceive the importance of the other former Soviet republics. Third, Kozyrev was too capitulatory and kowtowed unnecessarily to the West. Fourth, there was no domestic constituency for the Atlanticist perspective, except for the reformers themselves, because their concessionary foreign policy offered no short term benefits for the population. Finally, too little was being done to manage the concerns of the ethnic Russian diaspora now outside the Russian Federation.[14]

This combination of criticisms from the political center and right created a backlash in Russian foreign policy, and internationalist perspectives were increasingly replaced by "Eurasianist" ones. Variously called the "Eurasianists," the "post-imperialists" or the "Great Power restorationists," this group subscribed to five beliefs: Russian foreign policy should defend Russia's national interest, independent from

Western preferences; Russia should follow an independent course and, as a nation straddling the East and the West, become a bridge between them; Russia's top foreign policy priority should be its own backyard, the other republics in the Commonwealth of Independent States; Russia should not strive to achieve a full-fledge alliance with the United States, because it would become—to its own detriment—the junior partner in the relationship. Finally, in contrast to Kozyrev's emphasis on negotiation and conciliation, the Eurasianists believed that the use of force could not, and should not, be ruled out.[15]

The Eurasianist perspective had two major implications for Russian foreign policy in Asia. First, the definition of "Asia" had changed: Asia now meant Central Asia, with a renewed focus on the Russian diaspora and the Near Abroad (i.e., the former Soviet republics). Nothing makes this point more sharply than the argument offered by many Russian commentators that Russia's most important ally in Asia is Kazakhstan.[16] Second, with the new focus on Central Asia, China again became relevant, as China shares borders with three of the Central Asian states. This waxing toward China brought an accompanying waning toward Japan.

RUSSIAN FOREIGN POLICY TOWARD CHINA

Although the Eurasianist perspective supported improved relations with China, a rapprochement between the two countries also made economic sense for the newly independent Russia, as Russia today can no longer afford to maintain Soviet-level troop concentrations along the Sino-Russian border. For these reasons, Russia's relations toward China have grown increasingly friendlier, to the point that Yeltsin remarked in April 1996, "This pair of Russia and China, there is no other such pair in the world."[17] Indeed, the "constructive partnership for the Twenty-First Century"[18] has grown increasingly more comprehensive over the last four years, causing some Western analysts to express concern over the reemergence of an anti-Western alliance or a quasi-alliance between Moscow and Beijing. One author even talked of the possibility of a modern Eastern version of the 1920s Rapallo treaty between Germany and Russia, "two continental powers united by their real or imagined grievances against the West."[19]

The improvements in Sino-Russian relations began with numerous bilateral visits between leaders of the two nations. Kozyrev and Yeltsin visited China in 1992, and the two countries signed a joint declaration and more than twenty agreements on bilateral cooperation. In May 1994, the Chairman of the Russian State Duma, Rybkin, and

Russian Prime Minister Chernomyrdin each visited China on separate occasions, followed by Chinese President Jiang Zemin's September visit to Moscow. Yeltsin returned again to Beijing in April 1996.[20] These summits between heads of states mirror the widespread exchanges now occurring at lower levels: for example, 120 delegations led by Russian deputy ministers visited China between 1995 and 1996.[21] These exchanges have been fruitful for trade, security, and weapons transfers between the countries.

Trade between Russia and China between 1991 and 1993 nearly trebled, to $7.7 billion, with very heavy development of border trade.[22] Border commerce flourished so much that by 1993 Russian officials became worried about a large influx of illegal immigration and imposed stricter entry requirements and customs procedures. As a result, in the first half of 1994, Russian exports to China dropped 34.3 percent, while imports from China were cut almost in half.[23] This suppressed border activity negatively affected bilateral trade in 1994 and 1995, which totaled $5.1 billion and $5.46 billion respectively.[24] By 1996, Russia had lifted its visa entry requirement, and trade jumped 41 percent during the first half of the year.[25] This increase was further solidified during Yeltsin's April 1996 visit to Beijing, when Russia pledged assistance in building a $2 billion nuclear power station at Liaoning and the Three Gorges Hydroelectric project at Chang Jiang. Russia and China also agreed to cooperate in establishing joint ventures in pharmaceuticals and radioisotopes[26] and in jointly developing a Trans-Siberian natural gas pipeline from Irkutsk to Mongolia and South Korea.[27]

In the security realm, Russia and China have made headway on four issues. First, they delineated their 4,300 km common border in two agreements: the Eastern border in 1991 and the Western border in 1994. Although there have been some disputed islands in the Amur and Argun Rivers, both sides have downplayed these concerns,[28] and the agreements took effect after Russian Duma ratification in June 1995.[29] A similar treaty delineating the borders among Russia, China and Mongolia was signed in June 1996.[30] Russia and China also signed in June 1995 a joint border defense agreement to facilitate border guard exchanges,[31] and established additional protocols in July 1996 on border control, information exchanges, and joint drug enforcement.[32]

Second, in 1992 Yeltsin and Jiang signed a Joint Declaration on the Principles of Relations Between the People's Republic of China and the Russian Federation. This document commits the two countries not to join any political-military alliance directed against the other side, not to allow third parties to use their territory to the detriment of the other's security, and not to use force or the threat of force against each other. In addition, Russia and China agreed to begin a gradual reduction of forces and military activity within 100 km of each side of the border. Although China originally wanted this zone to extend 300 km, Russia refused because it would have required Russian troops to relocate in the Siberian taiga, without a supporting infrastructure or power supplies.[33] Russian troop levels in the region have been cut in recent years from more than 500,000 to 200,000,[34] numbers that should continue to drop (the twenty-first round of troop reduction negotiations occurred in October 1996).[35] The most symbolic agreement, however, occurred in 1994, when Russia and China pledged no longer to point nuclear missiles at each other and not to use nuclear weapons against each other first.[36]

Third, Russia signed a treaty in April 1996 with China, Kazakhstan, Tajikistan, and the Kyrgyz Republic to reduce and restructure military forces along their mutual borders. The Agreement on Confidence Building in the Military Field in the Border Areas stipulates three measures: (i) military forces will neither attack nor conduct military exercises aimed at each other; (ii) each state will inform its neighbors of any major military activities taking place within 100 km of the border; (iii) each will invite the others to observe military exercises, and increase friendly exchanges between border guards and military forces.[37]

Fourth, Russia and China have been developing direct military ties with high-level exchanges. In November 1993, Russian Defense Minister Pavel Grachev and his Chinese counterpart signed a five-year agreement providing for regular consultation between top Defense Ministry officials, direct ties between adjoining Russian and Chinese military districts, and an increase in military attaches in each other's capitals.[38] Moreover, since 1992, the two countries resumed cooperation in space exploration and in intelligence, which had been cut off since 1959.[39]

Russia has also been expanding its arms sales and military technology transfer to China. Each side has its own motivations for making this exchange; Russia is interested in earning hard currency and keeping its military industrial complex afloat; China hopes to gain military technology and equipment at bargain prices. By April 1996, Russia had sold China $5.2 billion worth of weapons, including twenty-six Sukhoi-27 (Su-27) supersonic fighter bombers, twenty-four MiG-31 high altitude interceptor fighters, and numerous heavy military transport planes, T-72 tanks, and other vehicles. China has also bought four S-300 air defense missile systems for testing and is considering the purchase of 100-150 more launchers, each to be equipped with eight missiles. In November 1994, China signed a $1 billion contract to buy four *Kilo*-class diesel submarines and four additional S-300 systems, to be delivered by 1998. Subsequently, China agreed to buy six additional *Kilo*-class submarines and had conducted preliminary negotiations to acquire twelve more over the next five years. In December 1995, China signed a contract to buy twenty-four additional Su-27s and receive the right to produce its own Su-27s under license. Some reports also state that China is negotiating for deliveries of the Russian Tu-22 bomber, and both the Su-30 and Su-35 fighters, which are not yet deployed in the Russian Air Force. Moreover, China is studying possible joint development with Russia of an attack plane called "Super-7," which will carry a MiG-31 engine and be built for joint export to third countries.[40]

Besides these arms sales, there has been a significant military technology transfer between Russia and China. China has sent between 300 and 400 of its defense specialists to work in Russia's aerospace research and development institutes.[41] Russia at the present time has little control over its military experts who possess state secrets, and many are currently employed by China. A Western diplomat, posted in Beijing, said that he and others often run into Russian defense industry specialists on the street whose presence was unknown to the Russian embassy.[42] Furthermore, the CIA has reported that the Russian government has lost control of its arms exports. The Russian government implicitly admitted as much in the summer 1994, when it expressed concern that China preferred to buy Russian weapons illegally.[43]

Russia's arms sales and technology transfer have increased concerns among neighboring Northeast Asian countries and the United States. Indeed, the arms transfer represents a potential threat to Russia whose government is aware of the risk. As a Russian Defense Ministry official noted, "Export is mostly limited to defense arms. This is a calculated move not to allow the military modernization gap between Russia and China to narrow down to ten years."[44] Although Russia needs the hard currency, it is unlikely that it will compromise its own security, especially if Yeltsin or another liberal regime remains in power. Despite some Western fears of an "Eastern Rapallo," Russia and China still have significant differences in interests, as objections voiced in the Russian Far East demonstrate.

REACTIONS IN THE RUSSIAN FAR EAST

Although the opening of the Sino-Russian border has had a positive impact on bilateral relations, it has created some resentment in the Russian Far East. The growing number of Chinese citizens in these lightly populated regions of Russia has raised concerns that the Chinese would take over the territory both economically and politically—concerns which have been aggravated by the region's increasing unemployment, wage arrears, electricity blackouts, and other economic hardships.

Most estimates of the numbers of Chinese citizens in Russia range from 300,000 to two million, although some sources claim the figure may be as high as five million.[45] One article states that there are 180,000 illegal Chinese immigrants in Khabarovsk Krai alone.[46] According to available data, each day as many as 5,000 to 8,000 Chinese cross the border into Russia, legally and illegally. This large influx of Chinese citizens, many of them tourists and street hawkers, makes it difficult for local Russian authorities to track their location and control their activities. Statistics from Russian border service officials in Morskiy Sbornik illustrate the problem. For example, 17,800 Chinese citizens in tourist groups entered Russia in 1994 through Primorskye Krai checkpoints, but only 10,600 returned to China. Therefore, 7,200 "tourists" remained illegally in Russia. Border guards were eventually able to deport 2,500 of them, but the whereabouts of the remaining 4,700 is unknown. As this figure represents only the Chinese who entered Russia through one krai during one year,[47] the total number of Chinese in Russia who have entered along the entire border is presumably much higher.

This growing Chinese presence has stimulated Russian xenophobia and racism. Although Chinese workers in Russia perform much useful labor in agriculture, construction, and light industry, the local Russian perspective has focused on the increased crime, drug smuggling, and threat to Russian culture.[48] Local Russians have accused Chinese traders of dumping low quality, even tainted, goods on the Russian market.[49] They have also registered complaints about Chinese poaching in border rivers and about Chinese attacks on Russian trawlers and merchant vessels on the high seas.[50]

A large portion of this concern may stem from a lack of faith in Russian business. Russians seem to agree that East Asians are good businessmen and, as a result, fear that the Chinese and other East Asians will quickly become dominant in the region if they open it too much. Siberia and the other far-eastern districts are thinly populated, while the states they border are overpopulated. China's economy is booming, while Russia's in this region is in serious decline. Huge armaments factories in the Khabarovsk industrial region have been closed, precipitating unemployment rates nearing thirty percent in some towns.[51] Furthermore, difficulties of transportation and communication between central Russia and the far-eastern regions have increased dramatically with the leap in fuel prices. Thus, many Russians advocate regional protectionism until Russian business grows enough to compete "fairly" with its Asian neighbors.

Local politicians have deliberately played on these concerns to generate local support. Yevgeny Nazdratenko, the governor of Primorskye Krai (Russia's Maritime Province), campaigned in 1995 for overturning the 1991 treaty which delineated the eastern Sino-Russian border.[52] He claimed that Russian interests were not protected during the border demarcation process. By that summer, Nazdratenko had joined with the administrative heads of Khabarovsk Krai, Chita Oblast, and the Jewish Autonomous Oblast (located in the Russian Far East next to Manchuria); together they decided to take matters into their own hands. They employed local Cossack units to protect their borders, declared areas under dispute to be environmentally-sensitive sites, and cracked down on Chinese traders. In addition, local representatives of the Russian special services sent letters to the local press claiming that Chinese troops were amassing on the border.[53] The Primorskye Krai Duma even tried to appeal to the Russian Constitutional Court, maintaining that the treaty was illegitimate. However, the Constitutional Court rejected the appeal in April 1996, indicating that Yeltsin planned to abide by the signed treaty.[54]

Perhaps the Far East politician with the most independent agenda was the former chief administrator of the Sakhalin Oblast, Valentine Fedorov. Fedorov, who initially won a seat in the Sakhalin parliament in 1990 by challenging Soviet colonial appropriation of Sakhalin's resources, directly challenged Gorbachev and Yeltsin on a number of issues. He repeatedly criticized the government for proposing to return some of the Southern Kurile Islands (Northern Territories) in 1991-92, and encouraged islanders to protest the surrender of their territory. Fedorov arranged to have his island's supply of fish sold by joint ventures to foreign companies and even hired a joint U.S.-Korean firm to explore gas and oil reserves off Sakhalin Island. When the Russian Duma awarded a bid to a U.S.-Japanese consortium instead, Fedorov tried to buck Yeltsin. As a result, Fedorov won widespread approval among Russian nationalists.[55]

With all of these regional problems, it is not surprising that there have been some calls for Far Eastern independence. Favorable references to the 1920 independent Far East Republic (FER) have reverberated as political slogans, and reprints of the FER constitution quickly sold out.[56] Regional identity coalesced in the November 1990 Siberian agreement, established by the chairmen of several Siberian krais and oblasts. By July 1992, all nineteen of the various Siberian regions and republics had joined the original group, evidence of the difficulties confronting the Far East and of the prevailing sense that the central Russian government did not understand these problems.[57] Although the economic conditions that originally united the region in 1992 still exist, Chinese immigration seems to tap a deeper emotional chord and has created a wider regional solidarity. Therefore, while Sino-Russian relations may seem rosy from Moscow's perspective, views in the Russian Far East will probably prevent an "Eastern Rapallo" from materializing.

Russian Foreign Policy Towards the Republic of Korea

Just as Russia's policies toward Japan and China have shifted back and forth because of domestic politics, its foreign policy toward the two Koreas has swung on a similar pendulum. As discussed in the first section, Russia's West-centric foreign policy stance in 1991-92 promoted good relations with Japan and the Republic of Korea at the expense of relations with China and the DPRK. In the case of the ROK, Russia's friendly stance merely continued Gorbachev's policy of cooperation with South Korea, which had led the countries to establish diplomatic relations in 1990. Despite Yeltsin's initial efforts, the pro-ROK policy has been muted, having brought Russia only modest returns and caused a serious deterioration in relations with the DPRK. Since that time, Russia has tried to balance its relations on the Korean peninsula.

Throughout most of 1992, the Yeltsin government followed a policy that consistently placed cooperation with South Korea above maintaining its relations with the DPRK. In March 1992, Kozyrev visited Seoul and assured the South Koreans that Russia had stopped selling weapons to North Korea and had ended technical assistance to the North Korean nuclear power program. When Yeltsin visited in November, he and President Roh Tae Woo signed a Treaty on the Principles of Relations. The treaty—which one Western analyst has called "the most important statement of Moscow's regional diplomacy since the 1950 Sino-Soviet Treaty"[58]—proposed building Russo-South

Korean relations on the basis of the shared ideals of freedom, democracy, and a commitment to a market economy. In a speech to the ROK National Assembly, Yeltsin stressed that while Russia was turning from the West, South Korea remained one of Russia's leading partners in the Asia Pacific region. Yeltsin stated that Russia and South Korea had never been enemies, although official dogma had kept them apart.[59] In a gesture of goodwill, Yeltsin also gave Roh the black box from flight KAL-007—downed by the Soviets in 1983 when it accidentally entered Soviet airspace near Sakhalin—and said that Russians "profoundly grieve over the deaths of completely innocent people."[60]

In the realm of security, Russian Defense Minister Grachev and his South Korean counterpart signed a memorandum in 1993 calling for regular exchanges of military and defense officials, military intelligence swaps, and the South Korean purchase of Russian military equipment.[61] The first military exchange occurred in June-July 1993, when a Russian delegation visited South Korea and a Korean delegation visited Russia. Moscow also sent a military observer to the ROK's Team Spirit exercises in March 1993, despite sharp protests from North Korea. In exchange, Seoul sent an observer to the August 1993 biennial Russian naval exercises in the Northwest Pacific. In June 1994, Presidents Yeltsin and Kim extended this cooperation with an agreement to prevent incidents at sea and to establish a phone hotline to facilitate communication on the North Korean nuclear issue.[62] In September 1996, officers from the Russian Defense Ministry and the Russian Pacific Fleet visited Seoul to discuss further military cooperation and arms procurement.[63] Russia has offered to provide modern weapons—including T-80U tanks, BMP-3 infantry combat vehicles, AT-7 antitank and SA-16 antiaircraft missiles—as a payment in kind for USSR debts. Although Seoul is not interested in large-scale weapons purchases because of the interoperability problems between U.S. and Soviet style equipment, the two countries wrapped up a $200 million deal in September 1996. Russia has reportedly offered to sell Su-35 fighter jets and MiG-29 fighters as well.[64]

One reason that Russia has pursued improved security relations with South Korea is the attraction of increasing economic benefits to both states. Russian-South Korean trade has continued to expand steadily, from $1.2 billion in 1992 to a record $3.3 billion in 1995, with Russia recording a $477 million surplus. South Korean firms have aided Russian factories in defense conversion, and some South Korean businesses have contracted to operate in the Nakhodka Free Economic Zone.[65] Academic exchanges and tourism have increased, with 100,000 Russians visiting South Korea (and vice versa) each year.[66] Perhaps most importantly, Russia and South Korea have discussed a $20 billion agreement to build a natural gas pipeline from Yakutia to South Korea, capable of exporting up to 45 billion cubic meters of gas to East Asian states.[67]

Yet the economic cooperation between Russia and South Korea has remained modest. To Moscow's disappointment, the steady expansion of trade has not been matched by a commensurate growth in direct investment in Russia. Only thirty Russian-ROK joint ventures had been established by early 1995, and overall South Korean investment in Russia remains at only about $30 million.[68] In addition, the $3 billion loan which the ROK offered Gorbachev in 1991 was suspended after only half of the funds were dispersed, and Russia has had problems repaying the $1.47 billion debt from the Soviet era.[69] These modest returns have caused great disappointment, as one Russian scholar remarked, "The Russian media has always mentioned the 'miracle of the ROK economy.' One of the reasons why Russia tried to normalize relations with the ROK was that the ROK could serve as a model for Russia."[70] For many Russians, the fact that Russia has not come further in resembling the ROK's model is a sign that the pendulum has swung too far. For these Russians, the modest economic gains from improved relations with the South were not worth the price of lost leverage over the North.

RUSSIAN FOREIGN POLICY TOWARDS THE DEMOCRATIC PEOPLE'S REPUBLIC OF KOREA

The price of improved relations with South Korea was a sharp deterioration in relations with the North. Some Russians have shown concern over this loss of influence in Pyongyang, especially after Russia was so obviously sidelined in discussions about the DPRK's withdrawal from the Nuclear Non-Proliferation Treaty (NPT) and Korean unification. This diplomatic marginalization has prompted Russia to reevaluate its policy towards North Korea. Now, in its attempt to regain lost leverage on the Korean peninsula, Russia seems to be courting Pyongyang and implementing a policy of "equidistant diplomacy."

Russia has allowed its relations with North Korea to atrophy in five ways. First, Russia has withdrawn its support for the North Korean nuclear program. In 1992, Moscow ended all official cooperation with Pyongyang in the nuclear field by refusing to supply the DPRK with nuclear technology and material. In October 1992, Russian officials stopped sixty-four Russian scientists from going to North Korea, which had hired them to help develop a nuclear weapons delivery vehicle. In 1993, Russian leaders strongly condemned Pyongyang's decision to withdraw from the NPT, and called on North Korean leader Kim Il-Sung to open his nuclear facilities to international inspection. In June 1994, there was a report, later denied, that five North Korean diplomats were expelled from Russia for trying to obtain nuclear weapons material.[71]

Second, Moscow has reinterpreted the 1961 Treaty of Friendship, Cooperation and Mutual Assistance to support North Korea only if it is attacked, not if it commits an act of aggression or a "provocative" act that invites aggression. In August 1995, Russia proposed a new treaty that eliminated any reference to Russian military support if North Korea is attacked. In response, North Korea postponed negotiations for a year, presenting its draft only in August 1996. The new treaty—which will be modeled on the Russian-Vietnamese friendship treaty—is now under negotiation, although Russia has said it will not contain a military alliance clause.[72]

Third, Russia renegotiated in 1994 the terms under which Pyongyang operates logging camps in Siberia and the Russian Far East. Although the camps earn Russia $57 million annually, Russians have been outraged by the North Koreans' brutal behavior toward Russian and Korean workers, and by their disregard for the environment.[73] During the Soviet period, North Korean secret police operated on Russian soil to control Korean workers and prevent their escape, a practice which the 1994 agreement ended. North Korean workers are now allowed to keep their passports while in Russia, which allows them to travel around Russia and to other foreign countries, as long as they have not committed any crimes.[74]

Fourth, Russia has virtually halted military cooperation and arms exports to the North. The two countries have ended joint naval exercises, although some military exchanges continue.[75] Nevertheless, Russian military contacts with South Korea are now more frequent, and are conducted at a higher level than those with North Korea. Reportedly, only ninety Russian military personnel remain in North Korea, and port visits and overflights have been substantially reduced.[76]

Fifth, Russia rejected the Soviet Union's trade policies based on barter and subsidies to the North. In 1991, Russia demanded that Pyongyang pay hard currency for its oil, coal, and food. Since barter trade with the Soviet Union had comprised half of the DPRK's total trade, Russia's new trade policies caused considerable hardship in North Korea.[77] Trade between Russia and North Korea plummeted from $2.4

billion in 1990 to roughly $100 million in 1995, and Pyongyang's debts to Russia now total 3.3 billion hard currency rubles.[78]

Soured relations between Russia and North Korea on these five fronts have significantly reduced whatever influence Moscow may have once had in Pyongyang. Isolated and threatened by Moscow's cessation of support, North Korea withdrew from the Nuclear Non-Proliferation Treaty in March 1993, using one of the few cards at its disposal to force other countries to negotiate with it. Following this announcement, the United States initially attempted to get other nations to agree to multilateral sanctions against North Korea. When sanctions failed, the U.S. was forced to negotiate. The result was a framework agreement, signed by the United States and the DPRK in October 1994, in which North Korea agreed to freeze its nuclear program, allow international monitors to inspect critical nuclear waste sites, and dismantle its main nuclear facilities. In return, the United States, Japan, and South Korea agreed to provide North Korea with alternative sources of fuel, including oil and light water nuclear reactors, which would be built by the newly-established Korean Energy Development Organization (KEDO).[79]

The fact that the diplomatic effort to resolve the NPT crisis was led by the United States and excluded Russia increased opposition to Russia's West-centric foreign policy. The Russian government was further snubbed when its first proposal in February-March 1994 for a multilateral conference to resolve the crisis was ignored by the other states involved. That Russia was sidelined from the process was not missed by the domestic press. *Isvestiya*'s Tokyo correspondent, Sergei Agafonov, attributed the lack of interest to the fact that Russia had become "an outsider" in Asia. In Agafonov's view, Gorbachev's unilateral move to recognize South Korea created a situation in which Moscow had lost its leverage on its other partners in Asia.[80]

The biggest slap in Russia's face occurred in April 1996, during the Cheju-do agreement for four-way talks on Korean unification. Besides the two Korean states, the United States chose to include China—not Russia—as the state with leverage over North Korea. As one of the two powers that drew the dividing line between the North and the South in 1945, Russia feels it rightfully should be the other power at the table. As Georgiy Kunadze, the Russian ambassador to Seoul, said in response to the Cheju-do four-way talks, "We've been dealing with North Korea for several decades—we know our way around Pyongyang. And this gives us an additional reason to think we can fare slightly better in dealing with North Korea than newcomers."[81] What makes the current situation so unpalatable for most Russians is that they recognize that they voluntarily abandoned their influence. As one Russian scholar noted, "In an effort to get something from Seoul, Russia cooled its relations with Pyongyang and put an end to its military relations with Pyongyang. . . . Then, what has Russia gotten in return? Its influence on Pyongyang has weakened, and it has lost a reliable military ally. And, Russia has remained a third party throughout the nuclear crisis on the Korean peninsula."[82] Instead of cultivating better relations with South Korea while maintaining satisfactory relations with North Korea, Moscow let the balance slip. Yet without its former leverage over the North, Russia has become largely irrelevant for other players in the region. To Russia's chagrin, it is China that is now regarded as the principal mediator between North Korea and the outside world.

THE PENDULUM SWINGS BACK: RUSSIA TRIES TO AMEND ITS POLICY ON THE PENINSULA

Russia's diplomatic isolation on the Korean peninsula reached its nadir with the Cheju-do decision to hold four-way talks with China—and prompted Russia to reevaluate its Asian foreign policy. Since April 1996, Russia has been trying to amend its policy toward the Korean peninsula in particular and Northeast Asia in general. Arguably, the new policy has three angles: restoring its ties with North Korea, pushing for multilateral talks in the region, and warming its relations with Japan.

First, Russia has realized that deteriorated relations with North Korea have directly translated into a peripheral role for it in the current negotiations. Therefore, Russia wants to restore its relationship with the DPRK—and hopefully also restore its status as a major player on the peninsula. As the Foreign Ministry stated in May 1996, "Russia is now in favor of maintaining more balanced relations with both parts of the Korean peninsula. . . . Russia will to some extent rectify its lack of attention towards the northern part of the peninsula in the past."[83] As a result, Russia has actively courted the regime in Pyongyang with two high-level visits.

In April 1996, Russian Deputy Premier Vitaliy Ignatenko led a delegation to Pyongyang for the first session of the Intergovernmental Commission on Trade, Economic, Scientific, and Technical Cooperation. During the visit, Ignatenko promised North Korea assistance in eight areas, including commerce, light industry, forestry, joint-ventures, construction, development of the Anju coal mines, supply of Russian oil for refining in North Korea, and the Tumen Free Economic Zone.[84] Russia offered technology and rehabilitation assistance for the Kim Chaek steel mill and seventy other industrial plants built with Soviet cooperation.[85] Russia also promised to consider providing assistance to construct a thermal power plant at Tongpyongyang and to explore North Korean oil reserves.[86] The Ignatenko trip was quickly reinforced the following month with a Russian State Duma delegation led by Speaker Gennadiy Seleznev. During his visit to Pyongyang, Seleznev announced a plan to deliver natural gas from Yakutia to North Korea, and presented Russia's draft to replace the 1961 Friendship Treaty.[87]

Despite big publicity and friendly overtures, Russia's visits received a cool reception in North Korea; President Kim Jong-Il was not even in town to greet the Russian delegations. Nevertheless, Ignatenko returned from Pyongyang with the "inside scoop." In interviews after his visit, Ignatenko described the North Korean leaders as bellicose and dangerous, stressing their belief in "the inevitability of war." He claimed that Russia's opposition to war helped to persuade North Korea to a considerable extent. The North Koreans "carefully listened to our positions," he said.[88] While Ignatenko's comments perhaps overstate Russia's role as the wise and well-heeded mentor of the North Korean regime, they attempt to give credence to Ambassador Kudnadze's pointed claim that "while others have been talking, we have been acting."[89]

Second, Russia continues to call for multilateral talks to resolve issues on the Korean peninsula. In 1994, Russia initially proposed ten-party talks, including both Koreas, the five members of the Security Council, Japan, the UN, and the International Atomic Energy Agency. Russia conceived of the international conference to address the nuclear-free status of the Korean peninsula, the normalization of DPRK relations with participant countries, and confidence-building measures between North and South Korea.[90] As Deputy Foreign Minister Aleksandr Panov said, "the Korean problem requires participation of many countries. If all concerned parties, including the United Nations, pool their efforts, a formula can be found which will be acceptable to all."[91] Since 1994, Russia has proposed eight-party talks, eliminating France and the United Kingdom from the original list.[92] Regardless of the number of participants, both proposals envision Russia as a major player in negotiations about Korean unification. Thus, Moscow's main purpose for this conference—like its similar proposal for a conference on the Arab-Israeli conflict—is to convince others that Russia is still taken seriously in Asia.

Third, in response to its stymied efforts at convening an international conference, Russia is trying again to warm its relations with Japan. For the most part, Russian calls for eight-party talks on the Korean peninsula fell on deaf ears—except in Tokyo. Japan felt as diplomatically sidelined by the Cheju-do four-way talks as did Russia, and in April 1996, leaders of the Japanese Liberal Democratic Party (LDP) proposed to South Korea that four-way talks be expanded to include Russia and Japan.[93] Since that proposal, Russia has tried to capitalize on its common interests with Japan. First, Russia announced that it would actively support the Northeast Asia Cooperation Dialogue, which comprises the two Koreas, China, the United States, Japan, and Russia.[94] Second, Russia and Japan both criticized North Korea's statement implying that it might take revenge on the ROK's October 1996 shooting of North Korean soldiers who infiltrated the South by submarine.[95] Third, Russian Foreign Minister Primakov has stressed that stronger Japanese-Russian relations could help stabilize the situation in Korea and that Russia and Japan are ready to "take an active part in a political solution in that region."[96]

Russia has backed Primakov's statement with a flurry of diplomatic activity. Until recently, three issues blocked Russia's attempts at better relations with Japan: disagreements about Japanese fishermen in Russian territorial waters, Russia's dumping of nuclear waste in the Sea of Japan, and the unresolved Northern Territories issue. Since April 1996, however, Russia and Japan have begun to address each of these issues in a constructive manner. At their April 1996 summit, Yeltsin promised Japanese Prime Minister Hashimoto that Russia would stop dumping nuclear waste into the sea,[97] and confirmed the 1993 "Tokyo Declaration," which called for resolving the Southern Kurile Islands issue "based on the principles of law and justice."[98] That same month, Russian Defense Minister Grachev announced the number of Russian troops on the islands had been cut back to 3,500 and he signed a bilateral security dialogue with his Japanese counterpart.[99] Russia and Japan continue to pursue resolution of fishing rights and the World War II peace treaty: the sixth rounds of negotiations for both issues occurred in October 1996.[100] In preparation for Defense Minister Radionov's and Prime Minister Chernomyrdin's Tokyo visits early in 1997, Japan and Russia extended their military cooperation with the opening of Vladivostok to Japanese ships and negotiations for joint drug enforcement.[101] These steps demonstrate Moscow's commitment to, as Yeltsin put it, "a comprehensive development of relations with Japan."[102]

Ironically, the new flurry of diplomatic overtures toward Japan—especially on the issue of the Southern Kurile Islands—has caused Russia to come full circle. In 1991, Russia's West-centric foreign policy team believed that warmer relations with Japan would help Russia to combat diplomatic isolation and curry favor with the West. By 1992, this perspective fell out of favor, replaced by the Eurasianist view that a China-first policy would reestablish Russia's great power status. Today, finding itself overshadowed by China and marginalized in negotiations on the Korean peninsula, Russia again believes that warmer relations with Japan will solve its problem of diplomatic isolation. Although back where it started six years ago—after a series of policy vacillations—Russia has remained consistent on one issue: its fervent desire to recapture its role as a major player in Northeast Asia.

CONCLUSION

As a result of its internal weakness and lack of resources to fund an extensive Asian foreign policy, Russia will continue to be viewed as peripheral by other players in the Asia Pacific region. The Russian Federation has lost many ties with former Soviet allies in Asia, but it has not been able to forge a constructive new role for itself in post-Cold War Northeast Asia. Russia's policy towards North and South Korea, as well as its circular journey in relations with Japan, demonstrate its tendency to take conflicting half-measures that fail to advance its standing as a major actor. Although Russia feels diplomatically and economically isolated, it has neither the resources nor the consistency of policy that would allow it to influence events in the region.

Nevertheless, Russia deserves attention because its continued internal decline could cause instability through increased arms shipments or nationalistically-driven border incidents with China. The Russian military still presents a considerable force in the region, albeit not to the same degree as during the Soviet era. Russia's attempts to restore relations with North Korea could also inadvertently be giving oxygen to the gasping Pyongyang regime. Therefore, Russia should not be omitted from the list of Asian powers. Russia's desire to be a major player in multilateral regional security arrangements has the potential to be a big stabilizing force in the region. This final point will become increasingly important as Korean unification becomes more likely, because Russia supports a nuclear-free unified Korea. Unlike China and Japan, Russia has nothing to fear from Korean unification but much to gain—as long as it is included in the process. Indeed, Korean unification may become the issue which Russia needs to redefine itself in the Asian Pacific region.

Undoubtedly, its current position is circumscribed by its weak economy and domestic political crises, but Russia has the potential to expand its influence significantly. Although it is on the periphery at the moment, Russia is bound to be, once again, a central factor in Asian politics.

CHAPTER SIX
UNITED STATES POLICY
AND CONCLUSION

Korean unification will be a victory for Koreans and for freedom. It will eliminate a viciously repressive regime and end the risk of war on the peninsula. A truly reformed North Korea would also be a major step forward for the region. Unification, or a real peace settlement, will, however, also give rise to numerous challenges to regional security. And it will put tremendous strains on Korea itself.

The previous chapters have demonstrated that change on the Korean peninsula has begun. It will probably lead to the unification of Korea or to a radically transformed regime in North Korea. Either outcome has traumatic and potentially destablizing implications for the region which could lead to the collapse of East Asian economic prosperity or even to war. The single most destabilizing change, however, would be the partial or total withdrawal of U.S. forces from the region after Korean unification.

The debate about America's proper military posture in post-Cold War Asia started several years ago. In a 1995 issue of *Foreign Affairs*, Chalmers Johnson and E.B. Keehn criticized "the Pentagon's ossified Strategy."[1] They argued that U.S. defense strategy in East Asia "ignores the profound shifting around the world, particularly in East Asia, from military to economic power."[2] They concluded that the real contribution of the United States to Asia was to open its market to Asian exports, and that Japan should assume a greater role in regional security while the United States diminished its military presence in the region.[3] In another article, in the fall 1995 issue of *National Interest,* Chalmers Johnson explained that the determination to keep U.S. ground forces in Korea until 2015 "directly contradict[s] long-term American interests."[4] Johnson called for a future with a well-armed Japan, a unified Korea, and no U.S. ground troops, with a balance of power strategy to keep the peace.[5]

Others have also called for a lessened American presence in the region because they see a decline in relative U.S. power and therefore call for a return to a "moderate multipolar balance-of-power system."[6] These analysts, such as Douglas T. Stuart and William T. Tow in an International Institute for Strategic Studies paper, argue that the growth of the Asian economies and of their armed forces mean that the U.S. military preeminence will decline.[7] They quote approvingly Henry Kissinger's statement that "[p]eace requires either hegemony or the balance of power. We have neither the resources nor the stomach for the former. The only question is how much we have to suffer before we realize it."[8] Thus, they claim that "[s]omewhere in the not-too-distant future the United States will no longer be in a position to guarantee the stability of the Asia-Pacific by its unilateral actions and forward military presence."[9]

There are also analysts who believe that greater burden-sharing could "ultimately" enable the United States to withdraw almost all its ground forces from Korea.[10] This would imply an air and a naval presence rather than the present force structure (which is based on a triad of U.S. ground, air, and naval units stationed in Asia).

In addition, as noted in the previous chapters, there will be forces at work in Korea, Japan, and China, in favor of the removal of American forces from the region. Korean nationalism after unification could lead to a desire to rid the country of American bases and soldiers. In addition, some Koreans might believe that maintaining U.S. military forces in their country would provoke China. Japanese pacifists might argue that the end of the North Korean menance would remove any remaining rationale for the presence of American bases in their nation. China's leaders are likely to see the unification of Korea as an opportunity to push for greater Chinese influence on the entire peninsula and for the removal of the U.S. soldiers stationed there.

An American withdrawal from East Asia, however, would be catastrophic for the region, and for the United States. Since the Korean War, three factors have made possible economic progress in South Korea, Japan, Taiwan, and more recently, China. The first is the combination of sound economic policies and hard work by East Asians. The second has been the U.S. policy of reopening international markets to Japan, especially in the 1950s and 1960s. Neither of those, however, could have been attained without a regional security order underpinned by the U.S. military presence in Korea and Japan. Besides defending America's allies against the communist states, the United States has created an environment which has neutralized Korean-Japanese animosity, protected Taiwan, and lessened Sino-Japanese rivalries. These preconditions for East Asia's economic progress are as valid today as they were two decades ago. (Disputes between Seoul and Tokyo over Tokto, and among China, Taiwan, and Japan over the Senkaku islands demonstrate how rapidly conflicts can emerge in the region.) Moreover, the American military commitment will become *more* important after Korean unification because the transformations in the international system will fuel suspicions and rivalries as states and domestic political factions jockey to take advantage of the new situation. Furthermore, nationalism may rise in the region as the old authoritarian systems of Korea, Taiwan, and perhaps China, are dismantled.

The United States is the only power which, with the assistance of its allies, can prevent these rivalries and hatreds from causing a breakdown of the regional order. The United States' ability to perform this task derives from the combined advantages of its power, its remoteness, and its alliances. Because it is the world's most powerful nation, America is stronger than any other nation in Asia, and, therefore has a unique ability to maintain regional stability. As a non-Asian country, it is not suspected of harboring territorial claims. For all the resentment of "Yankee imperialism," there is more concern in Asia about the ambitions of other Asian nations than of the United States. Some countries, especially China, might prefer to be the hegemonic power, but if they cannot have that role they would rather see the United States than another Asian state play it. Finally, the American alliances with Japan and Korea (and informally Taiwan) give the United States political and military ties with the region which are unmatched by any other nation.

The United States' commitment to the region is multifaceted. It encompasses military bases and security treaties, diplomacy, trade, investment, culture, human rights advocacy, immigration, and education. All these elements contribute to the ties that bind both sides of the Northern Pacific. But the foundation stone of U.S. engagement in Asia is the security relationship enshrined in the alliances with Korea and Japan (and implicitly in the Taiwan Relations Act). The tangible sign of this American undertaking is the stationing of American forces in Korea and Japan.

The American ground deployment is the bedrock of the security relationships between the United States and Asia. First, no other form of armed or diplomatic support is as influential and consequential. Soldiers are a more tangible symbol of a common destiny than ships or aircraft, because ground forces cannot be withdrawn as rapidly as naval or air power. Administrations can more easily put an end to naval or air deployments than uproot large numbers of soldiers stationed in local bases, thus lending a stronger sense of permanency to the U.S. presence. Governments can swiftly cancel rotating visits and joint maneuvers for political or budgetary reasons, but it is far harder for them to end a permanent ground deployment. Moreover, land forces require the stationing of combat aircraft for their protection, and of air and sea transports for mobility and supplies—thereby reinforcing the strength and profile of the armed presence.

In addition, almost all military contingencies still require the use of ground forces to fight or to deter wars. Even if U.S. air and naval forces remained in place, the absence of U.S. ground forces would seriously undermine the deterrent and fighting power of the United States in the region. American soldiers have a stronger deterrent value because they represent the world's only superpower. One country fighting another nation which is helped only by U.S. air and naval forces may think that it can escape a frontal clash with the United States. But no rational aggressor can dream of simultaneously fighting U.S. soldiers and avoiding confrontation with America.

Ground forces can be flown or shipped from the U.S. in an emergency, but such a tactic is far more difficult than repelling an attack if operationally significant numbers of U.S. soldiers are already in-country and need only reinforcements ("operationally significant" means sufficiently powerful to fight effectively for a long enough period of time to bring in reinforcements). Sadam Hussein granted the United States half a year to move men and equipment to Saudi Arabia, and let the Coalition choose the opening date for Desert Storm. Not all future foes will be as slow as Iraq's president. Moreover, moving forces into a theater can be provocative and inflame a tense situation; whereas, if troops are already in place, the visibility of measures needed to prepare for a contingency can be modulated either downward or upward.

The American deployment of forces in Northeast Asia makes it possible to acquaint American officers and men with Asia and for allied personnel to interact with Americans. It forces Pentagon officials to maintain close ties with their East Asian counterparts and to travel to Asia. One of the explanations for the success of the U.S.-led security order since World War II is that almost all American generals and admirals have served in Asia or Europe (and often in both). They are thus familiar with local conditions and know officers in other nations who have also risen to important positions. It is impossible to quantify the value of this personal element, but it is a critical aspect of America's ability to discharge its international military responsibilities efficiently. Living in a foreign country, training with its armed services, and playing golf or tennis with one's counterparts are often-overlooked but essential factors in maintaining strong peacetime coalitions. In addition, the U.S. Army deployment in Korea is the bedrock of the close cooperation and interaction between the ROK Army and the U.S. Because of the importance of the army in South Korean history and politics, it is most useful for the United States to keep in close touch with that country's military. Without the physical presence of their American counterparts, officers from Korea's senior service would gradually lose contact with the United States.

In addition to their role as a fighting force, U.S. armed forces have played an essential role since World War II in laying the foundations for economic development in Europe and Asia, thanks to the political impact of their presence. The American military presence in Western Europe and Northeast Asia allowed Europeans and Asians to regain confidence after the war and to feel secure that regional rivalries would not lead to new conflicts. The American military presence in East Asia (and Europe for that matter) still plays that role. Korean democracy is still in its early stages, and the U.S. presence gives it strength. The American military deployment also makes it clear to all concerned that a resurgence of Korean-Japanese rivalry cannot get out of hand. This American military role in cementing internal stability and regional peace is more difficult to measure than the purely military role of fighting wars, but it is as essential to the security architecture of the region.

KOREA

That United Korea could be unstable without American troops should now be clear. Korean politics are marked by a high degree of regional factionalism which could intensify after unification. In contemporary South Korea, regional loyalties are often at the root of party affiliation and political rivalries (as indicated by the results of the 1997 presidential election).

Moreover, beyond intensified regional strife, the reunification of the peninsula could lead to other problems. North and South Koreans have been socialized under totally different regimes since 1945. Northern Koreans may fear that Southerners will treat them as second-class citizens. Southern taxpayers could resent unification if they are taxed to pay for the North's rehabilitation. Alternatively, government policy could seek to avoid increasing taxes by resorting to deficit financing, which in turn could generate inflation or higher interest rates.

In addition, the assimilation of citizens of former communist countries into capitalist democracies is an arduous process. In Germany, four years after unification, over 19.8 percent (up from 11.1 percent) of East Germans voted for the "former" communists.[11] In Israel, Jews from the former Soviet Union created the first nonreligious ethnic Jewish party in Israeli history.[12] In Korea, the percentage of Northerners within the total population is far higher than the proportion of East Germans in Germany or of Soviet Jews in Israel. Moreover, the North Korean form of communism has been more extreme than the system in which East German citizens and Soviet Jews were raised. Therefore, the social, economic, and psychological integration of former North Koreans into ROK society will strain Korean society for decades.

These factors will make Korean politics more unstable and less predictable. The unification process will put great demands on Korean democracy, which is still in its formative years. Extremist philosophies of all sorts could emerge. Factionalism and instability in Korea would be a matter of considerable concern to Japan, the United States, China, and Russia.

The solution to all these problems will depend first and foremost on the Koreans themselves. The U.S. military presence will, however, contribute in two ways to preventing a radicalization and polarization of Korean politics.

First, the American soldiers will represent a sign of stability and continuity. Their power might deter extremists from acts of violence. Additionally, moderates will see the U.S. presence and the continuing ROK-U.S. military cooperation as a reassuring sign that Korea still enjoys the support of Americans and that the risks of continuing a democratic process are worth taking.

Second, if the United States withdrew its forces, China would try to bring Korea into its sphere of influence. The results might be factional disputes within Korea between supporters of different powers and the estrangement of Korea from several of its neighbors. In addition, without the U.S. military presence, establishing healthy relations with Japan would be much more difficult because Koreans would be more nervous about dealing with Japan outside of the overarching *pax americana*, and Japanese would be wary of a Korea detached from the United States.

JAPAN

The departure of U.S. forces from Korea would be a catastrophe for Japan. It could bring Korea into China's orbit and lead to tensions between Japan and its continental neighbors which would hinder trade and investment. The need for Korea to receive financial support from the United States and Japan is likely to keep Korea on a pro-U.S. course for several years. It is, however, possible that over the next five or ten years that an end to the U.S.-Korean military relationship could lead to a weakening of the political relationship between Washington and Seoul.

In addition, the withdrawal of the U.S. military from Korea could be a prelude to the departure of American forces from Japan. As the chapter on Japan argued, it would be difficult for Japan to implement an effective security policy without the advantages of a strong U.S.-Japan defense alliance anchored on the deployment of a significant U.S. ground, air, and naval presence in Japan. Without U.S. troops based in Japan, the Japanese government would probably have no alternative but to engage in a massive arms build-up. A large increase in Japanese military power would, however, create many problems for Japan. It would worsen relations with its Asian neighbors and create deep divisions within Japan over the course of defense policy.

CHINA

For the Chinese government, the departure of the Americans from Northeast Asia would offer an opportunity to bring Korea into the Chinese sphere of influence. In 1950, the Soviet and Chinese rulers interpreted American withdrawal from South Korea in the late 1940s as a sign that Americans would not fight for Korea.[13] Had the United States kept a well-armed garrison prepared to fight on the peninsula, it is almost unthinkable that the communists would have crossed the 38th parallel in June 1950.

After Korean unification, China will not attempt an invasion of Korea. It is probable, however, that China will seek greater influence in Korea, thus embroiling China in disputes with some Koreans, Japan, and perhaps Russia. A development of this kind would be greatly detrimental to regional stability in Asia and might even lead to a Sino-American confrontation as the United States sought to regain its influence and power in the region. Such a confrontation between Washington and Beijing would be very unlikely to turn out to China's advantage because of the imbalance in Chinese and America power. Moreover, even if the United States did not intervene to counterbalance China, Japan would perceive a growing Chinese threat and probably choose to increase its military power dramatically, the very outcome China wishes to avoid.

As a result, American withdrawal from Northeast Asia would be detrimental even to China. American forces in Korea close the option of Chinese political expansion in Korea and in doing so they protect Beijing from attempting regional hegemony which would backfire by generating hostility from the United States, Japan, Russia, and Taiwan.

TAIWAN

For Taiwan, a lessened American presence in East Asia would be disastrous. Taiwan has no formal relations with the United States, but the U.S. military in East Asia provides strong reassurance against any Chinese move against the island. Taiwan is likely to be particularly concerned about its security after Korean unification because Beijing would be tempted to consider that with unified Korea a reality it could now proceed to "reunify" China by bringing Taiwan back under its control.

An American withdrawal could lead some Taiwanese to accept the inevitability of Chinese rule and capitulate to the PRC. Others might conclude otherwise and decide that Taiwan should devote more energy to its defense, including developing weapons of mass destruction and ballistic missiles. A Taiwan without American protection might engage in a search for allies and give billions of dollars to any nation or group—be it Iran, Iraq, or underpaid Russian engineers and officers—willing to sell it missiles, chemical and bacteriological weapons, and nuclear explosives. Taiwan's recent dealings with North Korea are an indication of this possible trend. Such an outcome would be understandable, given Taiwan's situation, but could make East Asia less stable.

RUSSIA

Russia would not be as affected by changes in East Asia as would Korea, Japan, China, and Taiwan, primarily because it is first and foremost a European nation. Nevertheless, Russia has a stake in regional stability. Asian prosperity can enrich the Russian Far East, and instability is threatening for Russia, which is weaker in Asia than are China, Japan, and, in some ways, Korea. The U.S. military presence contributes to enforcing the territorial status quo, a policy to Russia's advantage. Because protecting Russian territorial integrity is not America's primary task, U.S. forces do not make Chinese inroads into Russia impossible; but, on balance, they make them less likely. America's presence may also contribute to lessening Russian concern that Japanese economic moves into the Russian Far East could lead to undue Japanese influence over a region which the Japanese Imperial Army occupied after the Bolshevik coup.

CONCLUSION

This book provides a framework upon which to analyze the issues which will confront Northeast Asia and the United States as Korea approaches unification. There are several major points which flow from the study.

First, the continued deployment of U.S. forces in Korea and Japan will remain the linchpin of the regional security order. It is possible that in several decades multilateral solutions will replace the present security system. In the meantime, however, the latent rivalries which exist between Korea, Japan, China, Russia, and Taiwan mean that the peace and prosperity of the region would be unlikely to survive a disengagement by the United States from Northeast Asia.

Second, besides ensuring a continued U.S. military presence, the major strategic challenge for Korea after unification will be the establishment of security ties with Japan. Japan is the dominant economy in Asia and has the strongest modern military in the region. A strategic partnership with Japan, as part of trilateral Korean-Japan-U.S. relations, would considerably improve Korea's security by allowing it to develop an alliance relationship with the largest capitalist democracy in Asia. It would also strengthen Korea's ability to make its voice heard in Washington by allowing Japan and Korea to combine their influence when dealing the the U.S. Congress and the executive branch.

The development of better Japanese-Korean relations will also be in Japan's interest. A unified Korea with hostile feelings toward Japan would be detrimental to Japan's security. It would lead to permanent tensions between Japan and its closest neighbor and could easily degenerate into a competitive arms race and push Korea toward China and away from the United States.

Improving Japanese-Korean relations is a long-term project. The recent development of low-level Korean-Japanese military-to-military contact is an encouraging sign, but much work remains. In particular, the inability of Japanese governments to deal unambiguously with the past has been a major obstacle. It is not, however, impossible to think that Japan and Korea could enjoy good, close relations. Poland and Germany now have strong ties. Poland is eager to develop military and economic ties with Germany, and to join the EU, of which Germany is the largest member. The history of German-Polish intercourse has been incomparably bloodier than that of Japanese-Korean relations, and territorial disputes between the two nations have encompassed far more land than the Korean-Japanese rivalries, which are confined to small islets and fishing rights.

The United States, as the major ally of both Japan and Korea, can play a significant role in establishing a trilateral strategic partnership between both nations. Nevertheless, the major steps will have to be taken by Japanese and Koreans themselves. America can facilitate Korean-Japanese rapprochement, but it cannot impose it.

Third, the financial crisis which hit Korea, and several other Asian economies, can be an opportunity to strengthen U.S.-Korean relations. South Korean economic policy made it very difficult for foreigners to invest in Korea. As as result, U.S. corporations and their Japanese and European counterparts have almost no assets in Korea. This state of affairs has deprived the Republic of Korea of powerful friends in the United States. If American firms had substantial investments in Korea (as they do in Europe), they would be more likely to use their influence in the United States in favor of good American-Korean relations when these are threatened by protectionist pressures in America. If the reforms undertaken by the new Korean governments facilitate foreign investment in Korea, it will considerably reinforce the ROK-U.S. partnership.

NOTES

CHAPTER 2 NOTES

[1]This gradual three-phase unification formula, a.k.a. the Korean National Community unification formula, has been the official position of the ROK Government. Despite some changes in wording, this formula has been in place since President Roh Tae-woo proposed it in his 7 July 1988 speech. President Kim Young Sam reconfirmed this unification formula in his 15 August 1994 speech. See James Cotton, ed., *Korea under Roh Tae-woo* (Allen & Unwin, 1993).

[2]These theories, named after a story appearing in Aesop's *Fables*, were hotly debated in 1993 when then Vice Prime Minister Han Wan-sang, in order to accommodate North Korea, made a short-lived proposal, entitled the Three-Stage and Three-Point Unification Formula.

[3]These contingencies are often called by different names: Crises and Lesser Conflicts (CALCs), or Smaller-Scale Contingencies (SSC), or simply situations short of war. See Carl H. Builder and Theodore W. Karasik, *Organizing, Training, and Equipping the Air Forces* (RAND, 1995); Chung Min Lee, "Crises and Conflicts Short of War: The Case of Korea," *Korean Journal of Defense Analysis* (Summer 1996), 31-54; and William S. Cohen, *Report of the Quadrennial Defense Review* (May 1997).

[4]Probably the first serious examination of various phases of collapse in North Korea that was written in English and circulated was Robert M. Collins, "Pattern of Collapse in North Korea," 1995. For recent discussions in this vein, see Kyung-Won Kim, "No Way Out: North Korea's Impending Collapse," *Harvard International Review* (Spring 1996), 22-25, 71; Kyongsoo Lho, "Reunified Korea's Challenges and Status" (Paper presented at the 7th KIDA International Defense Conference, Seoul: KIDA, 4-6 November 1996); and David S. Maxwell, "Catastrophic Collapse of North Korea" (Monograph presented at School of Advanced Military Studies, U.S. Army Command and General Staff College, Ft. Leavenworth, Kansas, 1996).

[5]When a cargo ship, the *Sea Apex*, loaded with rice entered North Korean territorial waters off Chongjin in June 1995, it was forced to raise a DPRK flag in violation of a previous agreement between the two sides. In another incident in August 1995, one South Korean crew-member of the *Samsun Venus* who took pictures of the port of Chongjin was arrested on an espionage charge and later freed.

[6]Prepared statement by Stanley O. Roth, Director of Research and Studies of the U.S. Institute of Peace (USIP), before the Subcommittee on East Asia/ Pacific Affairs, Committee on Foreign Relations, United States Senate, 12 September 1996. See also a USIP Special Report entitled, "A Coming Crisis on the Korean Peninsula? The Food Crisis, Economic Decline, and Political Considerations," October 1996. For an update of the food situation in North Korea,

see various reports by FAO and WFP on the Internet at URL http://www.reliefweb.int.

[7]Prominent exceptions to these majority views in the U.S. can be found in Selig Harrison, Ezra Vogel, and Robert Gallucci in contributions to various Korean newspapers.

[8]A number of high-ranking officials in the Clinton Administration expressed their concern over the possibility of an imminent collapse of the North Korean regime. They include John Deutch, Director of Central Intelligence, testimony before a Senate Select Intelligence Committee hearing on 22 February 1996; Gen. Gary Luck, presentation before a CINC Conference, 15 February 1996; Vice President Al Gore and Sen. Ted Stevens on their visit to the DMZ, quoted in *Chosun Ilbo*, 31 March 1997. However, some officials expressed different opinions, including former Assistant Secretary of State Robert Gallucci, as interviewed in *Munhwa Ilbo*, 9 January 1997, and former NIC official Ezra Vogel, in his contribution to *Chosun Ilbo*, 16 January 1997.

[9]According to John Deutch, former Director of Central Intelligence, "Inevitably the DPRK will disintegrate, unless fundamental changes are made from within, or a large amount of external assistance is provided." Gen. John Tilelli, Commander of the U.S. Forces Korea, who highlighted the volatile and unpredictable situation on the Korean peninsula, agreed with this statement.

[10]For an excellent detailed examination of the collapse theory, the reform theory, and the collapsible theory, see Larry A. Niksch, "The Prospect of Relations between the U.S. and North Korea Beyond the 1994 Geneva Nuclear Accord" (paper delivered at the Annual International Security Symposium of the Korea National Defense University, 22 August 1996). See also Amos A. Jordan and Jae H. Ku, "Prospects for North Korea" in Tae Hwan Ok and Gerrit W. Gong, eds., *Change and Challenge on the Korean Peninsula* (Research Institute for National Unification, 1996), 18-41; Edward A. Olsen, "The Roles of Major Powers in Creating Peace on the Korean Peninsula" (Paper presented at the 7th KIDA International Defense Conference, Seoul: Korea Institute for Defense Analyses); and Robert A. Manning, "The U.S. Position and Policy toward the Four-Party Talks" (Paper delivered at the 7th International Conference, Research Institute for National Unification, Seoul, 1997), 1-29.

[11]Jonathan D. Pollack, Young-Koo Cha et al., *A New Alliance for the Next Century* (RAND, 1995).

[12]Some 80 percent of the 8,554 respondents in this survey, conducted during the October 20 to November 7, 1995 period, said that they expect North Korea can maintain its regime; 56.1 percent said North Korea will undergo a gradual reform and openness while maintaining their socialist regime; 11.6 percent, Chinese-type reforms and openings; 11.5 percent, sustain their current regime. See *Chosun Ilbo*, 28 November 1995. However, two separate public opinion polls conducted for Sejong Institute in March and April of 1996, respectively, produced somewhat different findings: 63.5 percent of some 1,500 respondents said it would take a "considerable time" for North Korea

to collapse, but it would eventually collapse; 10.3 percent said it would collapse within one or two years. Only 7.5 percent said the regime would stabilize through reforms and openings. See Hahn Bae-ho, *Sejong Public Conscience Survey 1996* (Sejong Institute, 1996), 52.

[13]For a similar assumption about the major powers' role in yielding a unified Korea, see Olsen, "The Roles of Major Powers." In this paper, the author suggests that we think creatively about the possibility of an interim regime in North Korea.

[14]For a discussion of the roles of the four major powers in bringing peace and unification, see Changsu Kim, "Security Contributions of Regional Powers to Korean Unification" (Paper presented at the First KIDA-INSS Workshop on the ROK-U.S. Security Alliance and the Regional Powers over the Next Ten Years, KIDA, Seoul, 15-16 April 1996). Roles of these four powers in the early 1990s were discussed in greater detail in PerryWood, "The Strategic Equilibrium on the Korean Peninsula in the 1990s," in William E. Odom et al., *Trial After Triumph* (Hudson Institute, 1992).

[15]The Institute of National Strategic Studies, *Strategic Assessment 1997*, (The National Defense University, 1996) uses the term to refer to those who cannot challenge U.S. interests globally but are potentially capable of military challenges in areas close to their borders.

[16]For a similar argument, see William E. Odom, "How to Create a True World Order," *Orbis* (Spring 1995), 155-172, and Akira Iriye, "The China-Japan-U.S. Triangle," in *Can History Inform Policy-Making on East Asia*? (Johns Hopkins University, 1997).

[17]See Kim, "Security Contributions," for a conceptual sketch of the security contributions of regional powers including the United States.

[18]A recent discussion on contingency planning can be found in Robert A. Manning, "The U.S. Position and Policy toward the Four-Party Talks," (Paper delivered at the 7th International Conference hosted by the Korea Institute for National Unification [formerly, RINU], Seoul, 1997).

[19]After freezing the nuclear development program of Pyongyang in the Geneva Agreed Framework and its implementing agreements, Washington can pursue another follow-up policy that goes "beyond deterrence." U.S. Ambassador to Seoul, James T. Laney, first officially elaborated this idea in his speech on 11 May 1996. For a detailed discussion of the need for a major rethinking of our policy toward North Korea, i.e., the necessity to plan for a sudden change in North Korea beyond deterrence, see Don Oberdorfer, "Beyond Deterrence: The North Korean Crisis of 1997," (Paper prepared for the Symposium on Northeast Asia Security, Seoul, 16-18 April 1997.

[20]For the U.S. role in containing North Korean missiles, aimed at not only South Korea but also Japan, see Robert D. Newman, *The Future Role of the United States in Northeast Asian Security*, McLean, VA: SAIC, 1995.

[21]See Olsen, "The Roles of Major Powers," on the desirability to help build an interim regime following the Kim Jong-il regime.

[22]In his July 8 remarks before the Senate Foreign Relations Subcommittee

on East Asian and Pacific Affairs, he proposed to engage North Korea for the purpose of working to achieve a lasting peace on the Korean peninsula and U.S. support for the stated goal of unification on the Korean people's terms.

[23]He appeared at the same hearing with Charles Kartman.

[24]Michael Mazarr, "The Problem of Rising Power," *Korean Journal of Defense Analysis* (Winter 1995), 7-40. For a similar observation, see Kenneth Lieberthal, "The China Challenge," *Foreign Affairs* (November/December 1995), 35-49.

[25]USIP, "A Coming Crisis," 2.

[26]See Yan Xue-tong, *Analysis of China's National Interest* (Tianjin People's Publishing Co., 1996), 2. He maintains that "economic interest should top other interests and be followed by security, political and cultural interests."

[27]Wood, "The Strategic Equilibrium, 100.

[28]Robert A. Manning, "Disorder under Heaven," *Korean Journal of Defense Analysis* (Summer 1997), 131. It is interesting to note that some in Japan, though a mere minority in the open, are increasingly suspicious of the unified Korea's likely alliance (rather than just leaning towards) with China. This provocative view is hardly unimaginable, but it reflects the growth in uneasy feelings among some Japanese about the future of Korea. On the prospect for unified Korea's alliance with the PRC, see Hideshi Takesada, "Scenarios on Korean Unification: A Japanese View" (Paper presented at a CNA/KIDA/NIDS trilateral workshop, Tokyo, Japan, 13-14 February 1997).

[29]Olsen, "The Roles of Major Powers," 17.

[30]Nicholas Eberstadt, *Korea Approaches Reunification*, (The National Bureau of Asian Research 1995) 153.

[31]Hideshi Takesada, "The Prospect of the Relations between S. Korea and N. Korea Beyond the 1994 Geneva Nuclear Accord" (Paper presented at a security conference sponsored by the Research Institute on National Security Affairs, Korea National Defense University 1996.

[32]For a summary report from a Russian perspective, see Vassili N. Dobrovolski, "The Asia Pacific Security Dialogue Agenda," *Korean Journal of Defense Analysis* (Winter 1996), 101-16.

[33]Thomas Hirschfeld, *Multinational Naval Cooperation Options* (Center for Naval Analyses, 1993), 31.

[34]For more details, see Stephan J. Blank, *Russian Policy and the Korean Crisis* (U.S. Army War College, 1994).

[35]For an excellent discussion on definitions of hegemons and prospects for a regional hegemon by 2015, see David Shambaugh, "Chinese Hegemony over East Asia by 2015?" *Korean Journal of Defense Analysis* (Summer 1997), 7-28. He asserts that China will not exercise hegemony over Asia by 2015 and that it will possess neither the will nor the capability to do so.

[36]For an extensive discussion on key factors in the threat environment for a United Korea around 2010, see Paul H. Kreisberg, "Threat Environment for a United Korea: 2010," *Korean Journal of Defense Analysis* (Summer 1996), 7-109; and Changsu Kim, "Threat Environment for a Unified Korea 2010" (Paper

delivered at the Second KIDA-CNA Workshop, Seoul: KIDA, 4-6 December 1995).

[37]Robert Sutter, "China's Rising Military Power and Influence—Issues and Options for the U.S.," *CRS Report for Congress*, 16 January 1996, 38.

[38]Ralph Cossa, "The Shifting Balance of Power in Northeast Asia," in Patrick M. Cronin, ed., *From Globalism to Regionalism* (National Defense University Press, 1993). For an update of multilateral mechanisms in existence, see Ralph Cossa, "Bilateralism versus Multilateralism," *Korean Journal of Defense Analysis* (Winter 1996), 7-28.

[39]On current dynamics of Asia-Pacific security cooperation and their constraints, see Paul M. Evans, "Prospects for Multilateral Co-operation," in Desmond Ball, ed., *The Transformation of Security in the Asia/Pacific Region* (Frank Cass, 1995).

[40]Sung-Joo Han, "Korea and the World 20 Years After," *Korea and World Affairs* (Spring 1996), 8-21.

[41]See Kreisberg, "Threat Environment."

[42]See Joseph S. Nye, Jr., "Case for Deep Engagement," *Foreign Affairs* (July/August 1995) and Robert A Manning and Paula Stern, "The Myth of the Pacific Community," *Foreign Affairs* (Nov./Dec. 1994), 79-93. The latter foresee America's shrinking role, pointing to economic muscle and security muscle, and criticize the false idea of a pacific community.(82). They say further, "Not only do these conflicting pulls make the very term 'Pacific community' an elusive concept, but U.S. power in the Asia-Pacific arena is declining at a historical moment when the American stake in the region is rising."(80)

[43]See, for example, Manning and Stern, 89; and many books and articles by Ted Carpenter and Doug Bandow of the Cato Institute.

[44]For a recent criticism of exaggerated perceptions of China's economic and military potential, see Robert Dujarric, "Toward a Coherent U.S. Policy in Northeast Asia," *Hudson Briefing Paper,* Number 194, July 1996. The paper maintains that the U.S. should give a higher priority to the traditional alliances with Japan and South Korea than to its relations with China.

[45]When ROK Prime Minister Lee Hong Koo visited Beijing in the summer of 1995, Chinese premier Li Peng reportedly spoke of China's uneasiness over some Korean businessmen's alleged pro-independence actions in Northern China and their spillover into North Korea.

[46]A recent survey by *Joong-ang Ilbo* and the RAND Corporation reveals growing concern and worry among many South Koreans. For instance, on Japan's rearmament, 35.1 percent of the respondents said it would be a considerable threat, while 52.7 percent a very serious threat. See *Joong-ang Ilbo*, 28-29 October 1996.

[47]On 29 November 1995, the Japanese National Security Council approved the National Defense Program Outline for the post-Cold War era, which was later endorsed by the cabinet. The Outline shows that Japan is seeking a streamlined and hi-tech military; reportedly it identified North Korea and China as enemies, but later dropped China from the list.

⁴⁸Paul K. Davis, David Gompert, and Richard Kugler, "Adaptiveness in National Defense," *RAND Issue Paper*, August 1996. John Shalikashvili, "Joint Vision 2010: Force of the Future," *Defense 96*.

⁴⁹Jennifer Morrison Taw and Bruce Hoffman, "Operations Other Than War," in Davis, "Adaptiveness in National Defense." For brief case studies of developing countries representing peace operations, direct intervention, and disaster relief, and " nonstandard contingencies" concepts, see Paul Davis and others in Davis, ibid.

⁵⁰Yong-Ok Park, "Korea's Defense for the 21ˢᵗ Century," *Korea and World Affairs* (Spring 1996), 35.

⁵¹Nicholas Eberstadt, *Korea Approaches Unification*, 100.

⁵²Iriye, "The China-U.S. Triangle," 6.

Chapter 3 Notes

¹International Institute for Strategic Studies, *The Military Balance* (Oxford, 1996).

²See Gary L. Geipel, "The Future of American Atlanticism" (*Hudson Institute Briefing Paper* No. 198. Indianapolis IN: Hudson Institute, December 1996).

³Mary Jordan, "Japan Starts Building World War II Museum," *Washington Post*, 30 Oct. 1996, A25.

⁴To use Victor Cha's term in Victor D. Cha, *Alignment Despite Antagonism* (UMI Dissertation Services, 1994).

⁵International Institute for Strategic Studies, *The Military Balance* 1996/97.

⁶Conversation in Seoul, September 1996.

⁷James B. Crowley, *Japan's Quest for Autonomy* (Princeton, 1966), xvi.

⁸Richard Storry, *Japan and the Decline of the West* (St. Martin's Press, 1979), 130.

⁹Sydney Giffard, *Japan Among the Powers* (Yale, 1994), 94.

¹⁰Introduction, Peter Duus et al., eds, *The Japanese Informal Empire*, (Princeton, 1989) xii.

¹¹Ikuhiro Hate, "Continental Expansion" in vol. 5 of *The Cambridge History of Japan* (Cambridge University Press, 1989), 290.

¹²See Qunsheng Zhao, *Japanese Policymaking* (Praeger, 1993) and Chalmers Johnson, *Japan, Who Governs?* (W.W. Norton, 1995), 238-9.

¹³Tony Walker, "China, Japan Near $5bn Loans Accord," *Financial Times*, U.S. ed., 16 December 1996, 4.

¹⁴Ibid.

¹⁵See Robert A. Manning, "Burdens of the Past," *Washington Quarterly* (Winter 1994).

¹⁶Allen S. Whiting, *East Asian Military Security* (Stanford Asia Pacific Center, 1995), 4-6.

¹⁷Brian Beedham, "Tomorrow's Japan," *The Economist*, U.S. ed., 13 July 1996, 5.

¹⁸Kent E. Calder, *Pacific Defense* (William Morrow, 1996).

[19]See Julian L. Simon and Herman Kahn, eds., *The Resourceful Earth* (Basil Blackwell, 1984), especially the introduction by Julian L. Simon and Herman Kahn, pp. 1-49, and Herman Kahn, William Brown, and Leon Martel, *The Next 200 Years* (William Morrow, 1976).

[20]Harvey W. Nelsen, "Japan Eyes China," *Journal of Northeast Asian Studies* (Winter 1995): 83-5.

[21]Hudson Institute Conference, "Korea: Pivot of Northeast Asian Security," The Capitol, Washington D.C., 12 November 1996.

[22]Jurgis Elisonas, "The Inseparable Trinity" in vol. 4 of *The Cambridge History of Japan*, 236.

[23]Kawazoe Shoji, "Japan and East Asia" in vol. 3 of *The Cambridge History of Japan*, 434-5.

[24]Elisonas, 297.

[25]W.G. Beaskey, *Japanese Imperialism* (Clarendon Press-Oxford University Press, 1987), 42.

[26] Meetings in Tokyo, September 1996.

[27]Conversation in Tokyo, September 1996.

[28]On the pitfalls of foreign aid, see William E. Odom, *On Internal War* (Duke, 1992).

[29]John W. Dower, *Empire and Aftermath*, (Harvard, 1988) 309.

[30]Eto Jun, "A Nation in Search of Reality," *Japan Echo* (Special Issue 1995): 66. Originally published in January 1970.

[31]Norman D. Levin et al. *The Wary Warriors*, (Rand n.d [ca. 1992]), 50.

[32]For an account of the life of the first Tokugawa shogun, see Conrad Totman, *Tokugawa Ieyasu* (Heian International, 1983).

[33]John Whitney Hall, "The *Bakuhan* System" in vol. 4 of *The Cambridge History of Japan*, 150. The confiscation came to 13.2m *koku*, the *koku* being a unit of rice used to measure the productive value of land.

[34]W.G. Beasley, *Select Documents on Japanese Foreign Policy* (Oxford University Press, 1953), 48.

[35]J. Mark Ramseyer and Frances M. Rosenbluth, *The Politics of Oligarchy* (Cambridge University Press, 1995), 91.

[36]Ibid., 172.

[37]Giffard, 304.

[38]Ibid., 161. See George R. Packard, *Protest In Tokyo* (Princeton, 1966) for a detailed description of the 1960 renewal of the Treaty.

[39]Dower, 352.

[40]Introduction, Albert M. Craig and Donald H. Shively, eds., *Personality in Japanese History* (California, 1970). See also, Ian Buruma, "Becoming Japanese," *New Yorker*, 23 and 30 December 1996, 66.

[41]See Ian Buruma, "Becoming Japanese," 66.

[42]Ian Buruma, *The Wages of Guilt* (Farrar Straus Giroux, 1994), 61.

[43]See Thomas U. Berger, "From Sword to Chrysanthemum," *International Security*, (Spring 1993): 132-4.

[44]On MacArthur's cleansing of the Emperor, see Buruma, *The Wages of*

Gilt, 173.

[45]Thomas U. Berger, "From Sword to Chrysanthemum," *International Security* (Spring 1993): 120.

[46]Ibid., 146.

[47]Institute for International Policy Studies, IIPS Strategy Committee, "A Comprehensive Strategy for Japan," *Asia-Pacific Review* (Spring 1995)

[48]Kent E. Calder, *Crisis and Compensation* (Princeton, 1988), 24, 423.

[49]Peter F. Cowhey, "The Politics of Foreign Policy" in Peter F Cowhey and Matthew D. McCubbins eds., *Structure and Policy* (Cambridge University Press, 1995), 211.

[50]Calder, *Crisis and Compensation,* 423.

[51]Bill Emmott, *The Sun Also Sets* (New York Times Books, 1989), 210.

[52]Japan is not even in the top fifteen countries by international tourism receipts for 1996 (Hong Kong, China, Singapore, Thailand, and Australia are). Source: World Tourism Organization, web site. See, "Tourism," *Economist*, U.S. ed., 8 February 1997, 115.

[53]UN Information Office, telephone interview with the author, New York City, 4 December 1996. Total UN permanent staff as of August 1996 was 13,524, of whom 205 were Germans and 141 Japanese.

[54]International Institute for Strategic Studies, *The Military Balance 1996/ 97,* 294. Estimates Japan's 1996 peacekeeping assessment for 1996 at $229m, with only the U.S. assessed more ($475m), but Japan as of 30 June 1996, had only $8m in arrears vs. $889m for the U.S.

[55]For example, U.S. direct investment abroad on a cost-basis as of year-end 1995 stood at $39.2 billion in Japan, compared to $363.5 billion in Western Europe even though the Japanese economy is about half the size of Europe's. See *Survey of Current Business* July 1996, (U.S. Dept. of Commerce, Bureau of Economic Analysis), 47.

[56]*The Economist*, U.S. ed., 1 February 1997, 23, notes that de Gaulle once dismissed a Japanese prime minister as a "transistor salesman."

CHAPTER 4 NOTES

[1]Some of the contents of this chapter were published by Hudson Institute and *Internationale Politik und Gessellschaft.* See Robert Dujarric, "Toward a Coherent U.S. Policy in Northeast Asia," *Hudson Briefing Paper,* No. 194, Hudson Institute,1996, and "China: No Solid Foundations," *Internationale Politik und Gessellschaft/International Politics and Society*, No. 3, 1997 (published by the F. Ebert Foundation).

[2]See Chen Jian, *China's Road to the Korean War* (Columbia, 1994) on Mao's desire to throw the U.S. out of the Korean peninsula entirely.

[3]Mongolia jettisoned communism, but the Mongolian People's Republic was an outgrowth of Soviet power, not of Asian or Chinese communism. The North Korean communists, however, owe their survival in 1950 to Chinese intervention.

[4]Officially volunteers but in practice PLA units under Beijing's command.

[5]Conversations in Tokyo, Seoul, and Beijing, September 1996.

[6]Conversation with Chinese academics, Beijing, September 1996.

[7]Brian Hunter, ed., *Statesman's Year-Book 1996-97* (Macmillan, 1996), 790.

[8]Excluding Orthodox Christians whose communities in Africa and the Near East are unrelated to Western European colonization.

[9]Conversation with a Japanese scholar, Tokyo, September 1996.

[10]Kenneth Lieberthal, *Governing China* (W. W. Norton, 1985), 228.

[11]See, for example, Mary Clabaugh Wright, *The Last Stand of Chinese Confucianism* (Stanford, 1957).

[12]Arthur Waldron, "After Deng the Deluge," *Foreign Affairs* (September-October 1995): 149.

[13]Lucian W. Pye, "China," *Problems of Post-Communism* (July-August 1996): 6.

[14]Discussions in Taipei, March 1996.

[15]Conversation in Beijing, September 1996.

[16]Pye, 4.

[17]"Condemned to Live China's Great Contradiction," *The Economist*, U.S. ed., 14 December 1996, 61-62.

[18]Lieberthal, xv.

[19]Pye, 5.

[20]"Gang of one," *The Economist*, U.S. ed., 12 October 1996, 36.

[21]John Bryan Starr, "China," *Asian Survey*, 1 January 1999, 20.

[22]Pye, 4

[23]Kyna Rubin, "Go West," *Far Eastern Economic Review*, 10 October 1996, 60.

[24]See John King Fairbank, *The Great Chinese Revolution* (Harper & Row, 1986), 168-169.

[25]Conversations in Tokyo and Beijing, September 1996.

[26]Jie Chen and Peng Deng, *China Since the Cultural Revolution* (Praeger 1995), 19.

[27]Ibid., 24.

[28]Quoted in Charles. W. Freeman, Jr., *Managing U.S. Relations With China* (CA: Stanford University Asia/Pacific Research Center, 1996), 4.

[29]David B. H. Denoon and Wendy Frieman, "China's Security Strategy," *Asian Survey*, 4 April 1996, 431. The authors are quoting Lee in the *Straits Times*, 20 May 1994, 34.

[30]William H. Overhold, "China After Deng," *Foreign Affairs* (May-June 1996).

[31]See Douglass C. North, *Institutions, Institutional Change and Economic Performance* (Cambridge University Press, 1990), 34, for the theoretical framework of this argument.

[32]"Lessons of Transitions," *The Economist*, U.S. ed., 29 June 1996, 81.

[33]See for example Pamela Yatsko, "Another Way In," *Far Eastern Economic Review*, 5 December 1996, 63-66 on the widespread evasion of import

duties and sales taxes.

[34]Paul Krugman, *Pop Internationalism* (MIT Press, 1996), 181. Originally an article published in *Foreign Affairs* (November-December 1994).

[35]"How Poor is China?" *The Economist*, U.S. ed., 12 October 1996, 36-37. See also Roy L. Prosterman, Tim Hanstad and Li Ping, "Can China Feed Itself?" *Scientific American*, November 1996, 91.

[36]Conversations with several individuals in Beijing, September 1996.

[37]Keith B. Richburg, "China's U.S. Style Suburb Draws Few Foreign Buyers," *Washington Post*, 23 December 1996, A18.

[38]Prosterman, Hanstad and Ping, 95. Based on a survey of hundreds of farmers (63 percent did not know).

[39]Transparency International, "1997 Corruption Perception Index," www.transparency.de/press/1997.31.7.cpi.html.

[40]See Michael D. Swaine, *China: Domestic Change and Foreign Policy*, 29; and Ellis Joffe, "The PLA and the Chinese Economy," *Survival* (Summer 1995), 24-43; Lieberthal, 339; and Lincoln Kaye et al., "Disorder Under Heaven," *Far Eastern Economic Review*, 9 June 1994, 22-30.

[41]Mayfair Mei-hui Yang, *Gifts, Favors, and Banquets* (Cornell University Press, 1994), 99-101.

[42]Freedom House, press release, 6 May 1996. See also Kim R. Holmes et al., eds., *1997 Index of Economic Freedom* (Heritage Foundation, 1997), xxix-xxxii.

[43]See William E. Odom, *On Internal War* (Duke, 1992).

[44]Besides the work of Douglass North, see J. Mark Ramseyer and Frances M. Rosenbluth, *The Politics of Oligarchy* (Cambridge University Press, 1995), and *Japan's Political Marketplace* (Harvard University Press, 1993); Mancur Olson Jr., *The Rise and Decline of Nations* (Yale University Press, 1982); and Douglass C. North and Robert Paul Thomas, *The Rise of the Western World* (Cambridge University Press, 1973).

[45]North and Thomas, 6.

[46]Hilton Root, "Corruption in China," *Asian Survey*, 8 August 1996, 751.

[47]William C. Jones, trans., *The Great Qing Code* (Clarendon, 1994). See especially Jones's Introduction,.4-7.

[48]Ibid., 7.

[49]Robert D. Putnam, *Making Democracy Work* (Princeton University Press, 1993).

[50]Michael W. Foley and Bob Edwards, "The Paradox of Civil Society," *Journal of Democracy* (July 1996): 38-52. See also John Clark, "Shifting Engagements," *Hudson Briefing Paper,* No. 196, Hudson Institute, 1996.

[51]Lieberthal, 16.

[52]Pye, 5.

[53]Richard Pipes, "Russia's Future, Russia's Past," *Commentary* (June 1996): 33.

[54]See Charles Horner, "The Third Side of the Triangle," *National Interest* (Winter 1996-97): 24.

[55]On the Japanese Empire 1910-1945, see Chapter 6 of Peter Liberman, *Does Conquest Pay?* (Princeton University Press, 1995).

[56]Ibid., 114.

[57]Research Institute for Peace and Security, *Asian Security 1995-96* (Brassey's, 1995), 25.

[58]Michael Sheridan, "Entering the Orbit," *The Spectator* (London), 6 July 1996, 10.

[59]Stewart Lone and Gavan McCormack, *Korea* (Longman Cheshire, 1993), 15.

[60]Meeting with Chinese academics, Beijing, September 1996.

[61]*Freedom in the World* (Freedom House, 1996), 16-17. On a scale where 1-free, 7-least free, Singapore and Turkey score 4.5, Hong Kong scores 3.0, China 7.0).

[62]Frank Ching, "Danger Signals for Hong Kong," *Far Eastern Economic Review*, 17 October 1996, 36. Ching is quoting from *Le Figaro*'s interview with President Jiang Zemin.

[63]*The World in 1997* (*The Economist*, 1996), 87.

[64]Including coast guards (Maritime Safety Agency), Imperial Army and Navy veterans, and space spending, the defense budget is 38 percent higher (1996). Seventy-nine percent of the difference is due to pension payments for Imperial armed forces veterans. See International Institute for Strategic Studies, *The Military Balance* 1996-97 (Oxford University Press, 1996), 174.

[65]Depending on how the defense budget is measured the figure ranges from Y5tr. to Y7tr.

[66]Data from *The World in Figures 1997*, and International Institute for Strategic Studies, *Military Balance 1996-7* (Oxford University Press, 1996).

[67]Kent E. Calder, *Pacific Defense* (William Morrow, 1996), 86.

[68]*Forbes*, 15 July 1996, 258.

[69]Richard A. Bizinger and Bates Gill, "Viewpoint," *Aviation Week and Space Technology*, Washington, D.C., ed., 26 August 1996, 78.

[70]See Brian R. Sullivan, unpublished paper, on "low-technology" fighters defeating modern forces.

[71]See Zhang Shu Guang, *Mao's Military Romanticism* (University Press of Kansas, 1995) and Chen, *China's Road to the Korean War*.

[72]Conversation with a military specialist, Tokyo, September 1996.

[73]James Shinn in *Weaving the Net*, James Shinn, ed., (Council on Foreign Relations, 1996), 83.

[74]Pye, 10.

[75]Meeting with business executives in New York, July 1996, Tokyo and Beijing, September 1996.

[76]Root,756.

CHAPTER 5 NOTES

[1]William E. Odom, *Trial After Triumph* (Hudson Institute,1992), 7-11.

[2]Robert Legvold, "Russia and the Strategic Quadrangle," in *The Strategic*

Quadrangle, ed. Michael Mandelbaum (Council on Foreign Relations Press, 1995), 31-35.

[3]Odom, 14.

[4]Hung P. Nguyen, "Russia and China,"*Asian Survey* (March 1993): 288.

[5]Odom, *Trial After Triumph*, 25.

[6]Herbert J. Ellison and Bruce A. Acker, "The New Russia and Asia: 1991-1995," *National Bureau of Asia Research Analysis* (June 1996): 14.

[7]Renee de Nevers, "Russia's Strategic Renovation," *Adelphi Paper No. 298*, July 1994, 23-25.

[8]Alexei D. Bogaturov, "The Yeltsin Policy in the Near East," *Harriman Institute Forum* (August 1993): 6.

[9]Stephen Foye, "Russo-Japanese Relations," *Radio Free Europe/Radio Liberty Research Report*, 5 November 1995, 28.

[10]Legvold, 41-42.

[11]Ellison and Acker, 11.

[12]Ibid., 15

[13]Legvold, 42.

[14]de Nevers, 26-27.

[15]Ibid., 30-32.

[16]Legvold, 45. Kazakstan, as opposed to Kazakhstan, is the English usage preferred in that country

[17]Po Hua, "Russian-Chinese Relations as Viewed from Moscow," *Wen Wei Po*, 28 April 1996, A2.

[18]He Chong, "Yeltsin's Visit to China,"*Zhongguo Tongxun She*, 25 April 1996.

[19]Nguyen, 286.

[20]Zhang Rongdian, "To Develop Constructive Sino-Russian Partnership," Xinhua Radio, 10 April 1996.

[21]Igor Rochachev, Russian ambassador to China, interview with Beijing China Radio International, 24 April 1996.

[22]Legvold, 43; Ellison and Acker, 10.

[23]Ellison and Acker, 34-35.

[24]Po, A2.

[25]"Commentary on Li Ruihuan's Visit," Moscow Voice of Russia World Service, 24 September 1996.

[26]He, "Yeltsin's Visit"

[27]*Intercon's Daily*, 22 May 1996, 2.

[28]Dmitry Kushnir, "Gloomy Border Rumors," *Granitsa Rossii* (April 1996): 1-3.

[29]Anatoliy Yurkin, "Border Accord with PRC Tightens Security," ITAR-TASS, 23 August 1995.

[30]Grigoriy Arslanov, "Border Agreements Signed with PRC and Mongolia," ITAR-TASS, 24 June 1996.

[31]Yang Guojun, "Good-neighborly, Friendly, Peaceful and Tranquil Sino-Russian Border," Beijing Xinhua Radio, 21 April 1996.

[32]"Agreement Aims to Combat Drug Smuggling from PRC," *Rossiyskaya Gazeta*, 16 July 1996; and "Accord Signed on Border Cooperation with China," ITAR-TASS, 16 July 1996.

[33]Peggy Falkenheim Meyer, "From Cold War to Cold Peace?" in *Russian Security Policy in the Asia-Pacific Region: Two Views*," ed. Stephen J. Blank (Strategic Studies Institute, 1996), 6-8.

[34]Lowell Dittmer, *China Under Reform* (Westview Press, 1994), 184.

[35]"Disarmament Negotiations with Russia Held in Beijing," Beijing Xinhua Radio, 17 September 1996.

[36]Jiang Yi, "Sino-Russian Ties: New Constructive Partnership," *Beijing Review*, 13-19 November 1995, 9-11.

[37]"Epoch-Making Significance of the Five-Nation Border Agreement," *Wen Wei Po*, 26 April 1996.

[38]Meyer, 8.

[39]Stanislav Lunev, "On the Possibility of Russo-Chinese Strategic Cooperation," *Prism*, 3 May 1996, 12-15.

[40]For a discussion of arms sales, see Sergey Trush, "Russian Arms Sales to Beijing," *Nezavisomoye Voyennoye Obozrenive*, supplement to *Nezavisimaya Gazeta*, 25 March 1996, 6; "Sources Report on Russia's Arm Exports to PRC," *Tokyo Sankei Shimbun*, 25 April 1996, 1; Meyer, "From Cold War to Cold Peace?" 9; Meyer, "Russia's Post-Cold War Security Policy in Northeast Asia," *Pacific Affairs* (Winter 1994-95): 502-03; *Open Media Research Institute Daily Digest*, 8 March 1995, 2; Lunev, 12.

[41]Meyer, "Russia's Post-Cold War Security Policy in Northeast Asia," 530.

[42]Meyer, "From Cold War to Cold Peace?" 10.

[43]Ellison and Acker, 37.

[44]"Sources Report on Russia's Arm Exports to PRC," 1.

[45]Alexei D. Voskressenski, "Russia's China Challenge," *Far Eastern Economic Review*, 22 June 1995, 34.

[46]"One in 30 Residents of Former USSR is a Migrant," *Interfax*, 13 October 1996.

[47]"On the Homeland's Borders," *Morskiy Sbornik*, 19 June 1995, 18-26.

[48]"Customs Office Reports Increase in Smuggling in Far East," ITAR-TASS, 20 July 1996.

[49]Lee Hickstader, "Russians Fear Invasion of Chinese Traders," *Washington Post*, 18 May 1994, A1.

[50]Meyer, "Russia's Post-Cold War Security Policy in Northeast Asia," 505-6.

[51]Dittmer, 184.

[52]John Thornhill, "Russia Governor Challenges Border Treaty with China," *Financial Times*, 1 March 1995, 14.

[53]*Intercon's Daily*, 26 June 1995, 2.

[54]"Good Evening, China," Moscow Voice of Russia Radio Service, 30 April 1996.

[55]Ellison and Acker, 18; Sergey Sharayev, "Which Way Will the Islands Go?" *Rabochnaya Tribuna*, 5 October 1996, 2.

[56]John J. Stephan, "Siberian Salient: Russia in Pacific Asia," in *Pacific Century*, ed. Mark Borthwick (Westview Press, 1992), 505.

[57]de Nevers, 15.

[58]Bogaturov, 6.

[59]Ellison and Acker, 51.

[60]Meyer, "Russia's Post-Cold War Security Policy in Northeast Asia," 507-8.

[61]Charles E. Ziegler, "Russia and the Korean Peninsula," *Problems of Post-Communism* (November-December 1996): 9.

[62]Meyer, "Russia's Post-Cold War Security Policy in Northeast Asia," 508.

[63]"Russian Military Delegation Arrives for Three-Day Visit," *Korean Herald*, 17 September 1996, 3.

[64]"Defense Ministry Considering Purchasing Weapons from Russia," *Korea Times*, 8 September 1996, 3.

[65]Ziegler, 7-8.

[66]Speech, Kim Sok Kyu, ROK ambassador to Russia, in *Problemy Dalnego Vostoka*, 15 November 1995, 3-9.

[67]Alexander Krasulin, "Yakutia is Reaching Out for Warm Seas," *Rossiyskaya Gazeta*, supplement to *Ekonomicheskiy Soyuz*, 30 March 1996, 11.

[68]Vadim Tkachenko, "The ROK is Being Forgotten in Russia," *Choson Ilbo*, 6 March 1996, 3-4.

[69]Ziegler, 7-8.

[70]Tkachenko, 3-4.

[71]Meyer, "Russia's Post-Cold War Security Policy in Northeast Asia," 508-9.

[72]"Russia Confirms Negotiations for a New Treaty with DPRK," *Choson Ilbo*, 10 September 1996, 2.

[73]Ziegler, 7.

[74]Meyer, "Russia's Post-Cold War Security Policy in Northeast Asia," 509.

[75]Ibid., 508.

[76]Ziegler, 9.

[77]Ellison and Acker, 51.

[78]Ivan Zakharchenko, "Russian Delegation to DPRK," ITAR-TASS, 10 April 1996.

[79]Ellison and Acker, 53-54.

[80]Blank, 15-16.

[81]"Russian Ambassador 'Not Impressed' With Proposal for Talks," *Korean Herald*, 21 April 1996, 2.

[82]Tkachenko, 3-4.

[83]"Seleznev to Discuss International Issues on DPRK Visit," ITAR-

TASS, 24 May 1996.

[84]"Possibility of Improved DPRK Relations," *Hangyore Simmun*, 3 June 1996, 4.

[85]Hwang Song-chun, "Interview with Ignatenko on 13 April," *Choson Ilbo*, 15 April 1996, 8.

[86]"Russia Reportedly to Give Large-Scale Aid to DPRK," *Chungang Ilbo*, 21 April 1996, 1.

[87]Valentina Nikiforova, "Hard to Restore Trust," *Pravda Rossii*, 6 June 1996, 2.

[88]Hwang, 8.

[89]"Russian Ambassador 'Not Impressed' with Proposal for Talks," 2.

[90]Maj. Gen. (Ret.) Anatoly Bolyatko, "Russian National Security Strategy," in Blank, 33.

[91]Andrei Kirilov, "Moscow Fears Possible Crisis in Korea," ITAR-TASS, 3 April 1996.

[92]Meyer, "From Cold War to Cold Peace?" 12.

[93]"LDP Proposes to Include Japan, Russia in Korea Talks," *Kyodo*, 23 April 1996.

[94]"Four Party Security Dialogue Discusses DPRK, PRC, Japan," *Korea Times*, 11 September 1996, 3.

[95]"Tokyo, Moscow Agree to Set Up Defense Talks," *Kyodo*, 3 October 1996.

[96]"Primakov: Better Japan Ties Could Help with Korean Problems," ITAR-TASS, 13 September 1996.

[97]"Yeltsin Says Moscow Will Not Dump Nuclear Waste into Sea," *Kyodo*, 19 April 1996.

[98]Shin Nakayama, "Will Japan-Russia End Their Stagnant State?" *Mainichi Shimbun*, 13 May 1996, 2.

[99]"Tokyo and Moscow Agree to Widen Bilateral Security Talks," *Kyodo*, 29 April 1996.

[100]"Qualitative Changes in Japan's Stance on Kuriles," *Trud*, 5 October 1996, 3.

[101]"Yeltsin Sends Message to Japanese Prime Minister," ITAR-TASS, 4 October 1996; "Tokyo and Moscow Agree to Step Up Defense Talks."

[102]"Yeltsin Sends Message to Japanese Prime Minister."

CHAPTER 6 NOTES

[1]Chalmers Johnson and E.B. Keehn, "East Asian Security," *Foreign Affairs* (July-August 1995).

[2]Ibid., 104.

[3]Ibid., 107-111.

[4]Chalmers Johnson, "Korea," *National Interest* (Fall 1995): 67.

[5]Ibid., 77.

[6]Douglas T. Stuart and William T. Tow, *A U.S. Strategy* (IISS, 1995), 27.

[7]Ibid.

[8]Ibid., 4. The quote is from 1988.

[9]Ibid., 4.

[10]James Shinn in Shinn, ed., *Weaving the Net*, 73.

[11]"Germany: Survey," *The Economist*, U.S. ed., 9 November 1996, 16.

[12]How much of it is due to the Russianness of Russian-Israelis and how much to their upbringing under communism is, of course, impossible to establish.

[13]See "The Cold War in Asia" in Woodrow Wilson International Center for Scholars, *Cold War International History Project Bulletin* 6-7, 31-32 and 208 on Soviet and PRC desires to avoid fighting the U.S. See also Kathryn Weathersby, "The Soviet Role in Prolonging the Korean War" (Paper presented at the Conference "The Korean War: An Assessment of the Historical Record," Washington D.C., 24-25 July 1995), 4; and Chen Jian, *China's Road to the Korean War* (Columbia, 1994), 126.

BIBLIOGRAPHY

Allinson, Gary D., and Yasunori Sone, eds. *Political Dynamics in Contemporary Japan*. Ithaca, NY: Cornell University Press, 1993.

Ballantine, Joseph W. *Formosa: A Problem for United States Foreign Policy*. Washington, D.C.: The Brookings Institution, 1952.

Beasley, W.G. *Japanese Imperialism, 1894-1945*. Oxford: Clarendon Press, Oxford University Press, 1987.

Beasley, W.G. *Select Documents on Japanese Foreign Policy*. London: Oxford University Press, 1955.

Beasley, W.G. *The Modern History of Japan*. Tokyo: Charles E. Tuttle, 1982 (original 1963).

Beloff, Max. *Soviet Policy in the Far East, 1944-1951*. London: Oxford University Press, 1953.

Benedict, Ruth. *The Chrysanthemum and the Sword: Patterns of Japanese Culture*. New York: New American Library, 1974.

Bogaturov, Alexei D. "The Yeltsin Administration's Policy in the Far East: In Search of Concept." *Harriman Institute Forum*. Vol. 6:12, New York: Columbia University, August 1993.

Bolyatko, Anatoly. "Russian National Security Strategy and its Implications for East Asian Security." in *Russian Security Policy in the Asia-Pacific Region: Two Views*. Edited by Stephen J. Blank. Carlisle Barracks, PA: Strategic Studies Institute, 1996.

Bouissou, Jean-Marie, Francois Gipouloux, et Eric Seizelet. *Japon: Le Declin?* Bruxelles, France: Editions Complexe, 1995.

Bridges, Brian. *Japan and Korea in the 1990s: From Antagonism to Adjustment*. Aldershot, England: Edward Elgar Publishing, 1993.

Buckley, Roger. *U.S.-Japan Alliance Diplomacy, 1945-1990*. Cambridge, England: Cambridge University Press, 1992.

Buruma, Ian. *The Wages of Guilt: Memories of War in Germany and Japan*. New York: Farrar, Strauss, and Giroux, 1994.

Calder, Kent E. *Crisis and Compensation: Public Policy and Political Stability in Japan, 1949-1986*. Princeton, NJ: Princeton University Press, 1988.

Calder, Kent E. *Pacific Defense: Arms, Energy, and America's Future in Asia*. New York: William Morrow, 1996.

Calman, Donald. *The Nature and Origins of Japanese Imperialism: A Reinterpretation of the Great Crisis of 1873*. London: Routledge, 1992.

Ch'ien Mu. *Traditional Government in Imperial China: A Critical Analysis*. Translated by Chun-tu Hsueh and George O. Totten. Hong Kong: Chinese University Press, 1982.

Cha, Victor D. *Alignment Despite Antagonism: Japan and Korea as Quasi-Allies*. Ph.D. diss., Columbia University, Ann Arbor, MI:

University Microfilms International, 1994.

Chen, Jian. *China's Road to the Korean War: The Making of the Sino-American Confrontation*. New York: Columbia University Press, 1994.

Chen, Jie, and Peng Deng. *China Since the Cultural Revolution: From Totalitarianism to Authoritarianism*. Westport, CT: Praeger, 1995.

Chiou, C.L. *Democratizing Oriental Despotism*. New York: St. Martin's Press, 1995.

Cho, Soon Sung. *Korea in World Politics, 1940-1950: An Evaluation of American Responsibility*. Berkeley, CA: University of California Press, 1967.

Cohen, Theodore. *Remaking Japan: The American Occupation As New Deal*. Edited by Herbert Passin. New York: Free Press, 1987.

Conroy, Hilary, and Harry Wray, eds. *Pearl Harbor Reexamined: Prologue to the Pacific War*. Honolulu, HI: University of Hawaii Press, 1990.

Conroy, Hilary. *The Japanese Seizure of Korea: 1868-1910; A Study of Realism and Idealism in International Relations*. Philadelphia, PA: University of Pennsylvania Press, 1960.

Coox, Alvin D. *Nomonhan: Japan Against Russia, 1939*. Stanford, CA: Stanford University Press, 1990 (original in two volumes, 1985).

Copper, John F. *Taiwan: Nation-State or Province?* Boulder, CO: Westview Press, 1990.

Cossa, Ralph, ed. *The Japan-U.S. Alliance and Security Regimes in East Asia: A Workshop Report*. Alexandria, VA: Center for Naval Analyses, 1995.

Cowhey, Peter F., and Mathew D. McCubbins, eds. *Structure and Policy in Japan and the United States*. New York: Cambridge University Press, 1995.

Craig, Albert M., and Donald H. Shively, eds. *Personality in Japanese History*. Berkeley, CA: University of California Press, 1970.

Croizier, Ralph C. *Koxinga and Chinese Nationalism: History, Myth, and the Hero*. Cambridge, MA: East Asian Research Center, Harvard University: Harvard University Press, 1977.

Cronin, Patrick M., ed. *2015: Power and Progress*. Washington, DC: National Defense University Press, 1996.

Crowley, James B. *Japan's Quest for Autonomy: National Security and Foreign Policy 1930-1938*. Princeton, NJ: Princeton University Press, 1966.

Curtis, Gerald L., ed. *Japan's Foreign Policy After the Cold War: Coping with Change*. Armonk, NY: M.E. Sharpe, 1993.

De Nevers, Renee. "Russia's Strategic Renovation," *Adelphi Papers*. No. 298, July 1994.

Dear, I.C.B., ed. *Oxford Companion to World War II*. Oxford: Oxford University Press, 1995.

Dittmer, Lowell. *China Under Reform*. Boulder, CO: Westview

Press, 1994.

Doi, Takeo. *The Anatomy of Dependence*. Translated by John Bester, Tokyo: Kodansha International. Distributed by Kodansha Institute, 1981 (original 1973).

Dower, John W. *Empire and Aftermath: Yoshida Shigeru and the Japanese Experience, 1878-1954*. Cambridge, MA: Council on East Asian Studies, Harvard University: Harvard University Press, 1988.

Dreyer, June Teufel. *China's Strategic View: The Role of the People's Liberation Army*. Carlisle Barracks, PA: Strategic Studies Institute, U.S. Army War College, 1996.

Duus, Peter. *Party Rivalry and Political Change in Taisho Japan*. Cambridge MA: Harvard University Press, 1968.

Duus, Peter, Ramon H. Myers, and Mark R. Peattie, eds. *The Japanese Wartime Empire, 1931-1945*. Princeton, NJ: Princeton University Press, 1996.

Duus, Peter, Ramon H. Myers, and Mark R. Peattie, eds. *The Japanese Informal Empire in China, 1895-1937*. Princeton, NJ: Princeton University Press, 1989.

Eberstadt, Nicholas. *Korea Approaches Reunification*. Armonk, NY: M.E. Sharpe, 1995.

Eckert, Carter J. et. al., *Korea: Old and New: A History*. Cambridge, MA: Harvard University Press, Korea Institute, 1990.

Economist Intelligence Unit. *Country Profiles*. London: *The Economist*. "The World in 1997." *The Economist,* London, 1996.

Ellison, Herbert J., and Bruce A. Acker. "The New Russia and Asia: 1991-1995," *National Bureau of Asia Research Analysis*. Vol. 7:1,1-64, Seattle, WA, June 1996.

Emmott, Bill. *The Sun Also Sets: The Limits to Japan's Economic Power*. New York: Times Books, 1989.

Fairbank, John King. *The United States and China*. 4th ed. enl., Cambridge, MA: Harvard University Press, 1983.

Fallows, James. *Looking at the Sun: The Rise of the New East Asian Economic and Political System*. New York: Pantheon Books, 1994.

Faust, John R., and Judith F. Kornberg. *China in World Politics*. Boulder, CO: Lynne Reinner Publishers, 1995.

Feigenbaum, Evan A. *Change in Taiwan and Potential Adversity in the Strait*. Santa Monica, CA: RAND Corporation, 1995.

Feuerwerker, Albert. *Studies in the Economic History of Late Imperial China: Handicraft, Modern Industry, & the State*. Ann Arbor, MI: Center for Chinese Studies, The University of Michigan, 1995.

Finkelstein, David M. *Washington's Taiwan Dilemma, 1949-1950: From Abandonment to Salvation*. Fairfax, VA: George Mason University Press, 1993.

Finn, Richard B. *Winners in Peace: MacArthur, Yoshida, and Postwar Japan*. Berkeley, CA: University of California Press, 1992.

Fogel, Joshua A. *Politics and Sinology: The Case of Naito Konan (1866-1934).* Cambridge, MA: Harvard University Press, Council on East Asian Studies, 1984.

Foye, Stephen. "Russo-Japanese Relations: Still Traveling a Rocky Road." *Radio Free Europe/ Radio Liberty Research Report,* Vol. 2:44, (5 November 1995): 27-34.

Freeman, Charles W. *Managing U.S. Relations With China.* Stanford, CA: Asia/Pacific Research Center, Stanford University, 1996.

Fu, Jen-kun. *Taiwan and the Geopolitics of the Asian-American Dilemma.* New York: Praeger, 1992.

Fukuyama, Francis, and Kongdan Oh. *The U.S.-Japan Security Relationship After the Cold War.* Santa Monica, CA: RAND, 1993.

Fukuzawa Yukichi. *The Autobiography of Yukichi Fukuzawa.* Revised translation by Eiichi Kiyooka. New York: Columbia University Press, 1966.

Funabashi, Yoichi. *Asia Pacific Fusion: Japan's Role in APEC.* Washington, DC: Institute for International Economics, 1995.

Gao, Shangquan. *China's Economic Reform.* New York: St. Martin's Press, 1996.

Garver, John W. *Foreign Relations of the People's Republic of China.* Englewood Cliffs, NJ: Prentice Hall, 1993.

Geipel, Gary L. *The Future of American Atlanticism. Hudson Briefing Paper,* No. 198, Indianapolis, IN: Hudson Institute, December 1996.

Gelman, Harry. *Russo-Japanese Relations and the Future of the U.S.-Japanese Alliance.* Santa Monica, CA: RAND Corporation, 1993.

Giffard, Sydney. *Japan Among the Powers 1890-1990.* New Haven CT: Yale University Press, 1994.

Gittings, John. *China Changes Face: The Road from Revolution 1949-1989.* Oxford: Oxford University Press, 1989.

Gittings, John. *The World and China, 1922-1972.* New York: Harper & Row, 1974.

Gluck, Carol, and Stephen R. Graubard, eds. *Showa: The Japan of Hirohito.* New York: Norton, 1992.

Goncharov, Sergei N., John W. Lewis, and Xue Litai. *Uncertain Partners: Stalin, Mao, and the Korean War.* Stanford, CA: Stanford University Press, 1993.

Gong, Gerrit W., Seizaburo Sato, and Tae Hwan Ok, eds. *Korean Peninsula Developments and U.S.-Japan-South Korea Relations.* 3 vols. Washington, DC: Center for Strategic and International Studies, 1993-94.

Gordon, Andrew, ed. *Postwar Japan as History.* Berkeley, CA: University of California Press, 1993.

Gu, Weiqun. *Conflicts of Divided Nations: The Cases of China and Korea.* Westport, CT: Praeger, 1995.

Hackett, Roger F. *Yamagata Arimoto in the Rise of Modern Japan,*

1838-1922. Cambridge, MA: Harvard University Press, 1971.

Haggard, Stephan and Robert R. Kaufman. *The Political Economy of Democratic Transitions.* Princeton, NJ: Princeton University Press, 1995.

Hall, John Whitney, ed. *The Cambridge History of Japan,* vol. 4, *Early Modern Japan.* Cambridge, MA: Cambridge University Press, 1991.

Hane, Mikiso. *Premodern Japan: A Historical Survey.* Boulder, CO: Westview Press, 1991.

Holmes, Kim, Bryan T. Johnson, and Melanie Kirkpatrick, eds. *1997 Index of Economic Freedom.* Washington, DC: Heritage Foundation, Dow Jones, 1997.

Hsiung, James C., ed. *Asia Pacific in the New World Politics.* Boulder, CO: Lynne Rienner Publishers, 1993.

Hunt, Michael H. and Niu Jun. *Toward a History of Chinese Communist Foreign Relations 1920s-1960s: Personalities and Interpretive Approaches.* Washington, DC: Woodrow Wilson Center, Asia Program, 1992.

Huntington, Samuel P. *The Soldier and the State: The Theory and Politics of Civil-Military Relations.* Cambridge, MA: Harvard University Press, Belknap Press, 1981 (original 1957).

Huntington, Samuel P. *The Third Wave: Democratization in the Late Twentieth Century.* Norman, OK: University of Oklahoma Press, 1991.

Huntington, Samuel P. *The Clash of Civilizations and the Remaking of the World Order.* New York: Simon & Schuster, 1996.

Inoguchi, Takashi. *Japan's Foreign Policy in an Era of Global Change.* New York: St. Martin's Press, 1993.

International Institute for Strategic Studies. *The Military Balance, 1996-1997.* Oxford: Oxford University Press, International Institute for Strategic Studies, 1996.

International Monetary Fund. *World Economic Outlook, a Survey.* Washington, DC: International Monetary Fund, 1996.

Iriye, Akira. *Across the Pacific: An Inner History of American-East Asian Relations.* New York: Harcourt, Brace & World, 1967.

Iriye, Akira. *China and Japan in the Global Setting.* Cambridge, MA: Harvard University Press, 1992.

Iriye, Akira. *The Cold War in Asia: A Historical Introduction.* Englewood Cliffs, NJ: Prentice-Hall, 1974.

Iriye, Akira. *The Origins of the Second World War in Asia and the Pacific.* London: Longman, 1987.

Iriye, Akira, ed. *The Chinese and the Japanese: Essays in Political and Cultural Interactions.* Princeton, NJ: Princeton University Press, 1980.

Irokawa, Daikichi. *The Age of Hirohito: In Search of Modern Japan.* New York: Free Press, 1995.

Jacobson, David ed. *Old Nations, New World: Conceptions of World*

Order. Boulder, CO: Westview Press, 1994.

Jansen, Marius B. *China in the Tokugawa World*. Cambridge, MA: Harvard University Press, 1992.

Jansen, Marius B. *Japan and China: From War to Peace, 1894-1972*. Chicago, IL: Rand McNally College Publishing, 1975.

Jansen, Marius B. *The Japanese and Sun Yat-sen*. Cambridge, MA: Harvard University Press, 1954.

Jansen, Marius B., ed. *The Cambridge History of Japan*, vol. 5, *The Nineteenth Century*. Cambridge, MA: Cambridge University Press, 1989.

Johnson, Chalmers. *Japan: Who Governs? The Rise of the Developmental State*. New York: Norton, 1995.

Johnston, Alastair Iain. *Cultural Realism: Strategic Culture and Grand Strategy in Chinese History*. Princeton, NJ: Princeton University Press, 1995.

Jones, Eric, Lionel Frost, and Colin White. *Coming Full Circle: An Economic History of the Pacific Rim*. Boulder, CO: Westview Press, 1993.

Jones, William C., trans. *The Great Qing Code*. With assistance of Tianquan Cheng and Yongling Jiang. Oxford: Clarendon Press, 1994.

Kahn, Herman, William Brown, and Leon Martel. *The Next 200 Years: A Scenario for America and the World*. With assistance of Hudson Institute staff. New York: Morrow, 1976.

Katzenstein, Peter J. and Nobuo Okawara. *Japan's National Security: Structures, Norms and Policy Responses in a Changing World*. Ithaca, NY: East Asia Program, Cornell University, 1993.

Keddel, Joseph P. *The Politics of Defense in Japan: Managing Internal and External Pressures*. Armonk, NY: M.E. Sharpe, 1993.

Kerbo, Harold R. and John A. McKinstry. *Who Rules Japan? The Inner Circles of Economic and Political Power*. Westport, CT: Praeger, 1995.

Khalilzad, Zalmay M., ed. *Strategic Appraisal 1996*. Santa Monica, CA: RAND Corporation, 1996.

Kihl, Young Whan, ed. *Korea and the World: Beyond the Cold War*. Boulder, CO: Westview Press, 1994.

Kim, Key-Hiuk. *The Last Phase of the East Asian World Order: Korea, Japan, and the Chinese Empire, 1860-1882*. Berkeley, CA: University of California Press, 1980.

Kosai Yutaka. *The Era of High-Speed Growth: Notes on the Postwar Japanese Economy*. Translated by Jacqueline Kaminski. Tokyo: University of Tokyo Press, 1986.

Krepinevich, Andrew F. *The Conflict Environment of 2016: A Scenario-Based Approach*. Washington, DC: Center for Strategic and Budgetary Assessments, 1996.

Krugman, Paul. *Pop Internationalism*. Cambridge, MA: MIT Press, 1996.

Kuno, Yoshi S. *Japanese Expansion on the Asiatic Continent: A Study in the History of Japan with Special Reference to Her International Relations with China, Korea, and Russia,* vols. I and II. Berkeley, CA: University of California Press, 1937-1940.

Lane, Kevin P. *Sovereignty and the Status Quo: The Historical Roots of China's Hong Kong Policy.* Boulder, CO: Westview Press, 1990.

Lasater, Martin L. *The Changing of the Guard: President Clinton and the Security of Taiwan.* Boulder, CO: Westview Press, 1995.

Lee Chae-jin. *China and Korea: Dynamic Relations.* In collaboration with Doo-bok Park. Stanford, CA: Hoover Institution Press, 1996.

Lee, Chae-Lin and Hideo Sato, eds. *U.S.-Japan Partnership in Conflict Management: The Case of Korea.* Claremont, CA: Keck Center for International and Strategic Studies, Claremont McKenna College, 1993.

Lee, Khoon Choy. *Japan: Between Myth and Reality.* Singapore: World Scientific, 1995.

Legvold, Robert. *The Collapse of the Soviet Union and the New Asian Order.* NBR Analysis Series, Vol. 3:4. Seattle, WA: National Bureau of Asian Research, 1992.

Leonard, Jane Kate and John R. Watt, eds. *To Achieve Security and Wealth: The Qing Imperial State and the Economy, 1644-1911.* Ithaca, NY: East Asia Program, Cornell University, 1992.

Levin, Norman D., Mark Lorell, and Arthur Alexander. *The Wary Warriors: Future Directions in Japanese Security Policies.* Santa Monica, CA: RAND Corporation, for the United States Air Force, 1993.

Liberman, Peter. *Does Conquest Pay? The Exploitation of Occupied Industrial Societies.* Princeton, NJ: Princeton University Press, 1996.

Lone, Stewart and Gavan McCormack. *Korea Since 1850.* New York: St. Martin's Press, 1993.

Lowe, Peter. *The Origins of the Korean War.* London: Longman, 1986.

Macdonald, Donald Stone. *The Koreans: Contemporary Politics and Society.* Boulder, CO: Westview Press, 1988.

Macdonald, Donald Stone. *U.S.-Korean Relations from Liberation to Self-Reliance: The Twenty-Year Record: an Interpretative Summary of the Archives of the U.S. Department of State for the Period 1945-1965.* Boulder, CO: Westview Press, 1992.

Mandelbaum, Michael, ed. *The Strategic Quadrangle: Russia, China, Japan and the United States in East Asia.* New York: Council on Foreign Relations Press, 1995.

Mao, Tse-tung (Zedong). *Basic Tactics.* Edited and translated by Stuart R. Schram. London: Pall Mall Press, 1967.

Maruyama Masao. *Thought and Behaviour in Modern Japanese Politics.* London: Oxford University Press, 1966.

Mass, Jeffrey P. and William B. Hauser, eds. *The Bakufu in Japanese*

History. Stanford, CA: Stanford University Press, 1985.

Masumi Junnosuke. *Contemporary Politics in Japan.* Translated by Lonny E. Carlile. Berkeley, CA: University of California Press, 1995.

Matray, James Irving. *The Reluctant Crusade: American Foreign Policy in Korea, 1941-1950.* Honolulu, HI: University of Hawaii Press, 1985.

McNeil, Frank. *Japanese Politics: Decay or Reform?: The Consequences of Political Stagnation and the Prospects for Major Change.* Washington, DC: Carnegie Endowment for International Peace, 1993.

Meyer, Peggy Falkenheim. "From Cold War to Cold Peace?" in *Russian Security Policy in the Asia-Pacific Region: Two Views.* Edited by Stephen J. Blank. Carlisle Barracks, PA: Strategic Studies Institute, 1996.

Millar, T.B. and James Walter, eds. *Asian-Pacific Security After the Cold War,* 2nd ed. Camberra, ACT: Allen & Unwin in association with the Department of International Relations, 1993.

Mochizuki, Mike M. *Japan: Domestic Change and Foreign Policy.* Santa Monica, CA: RAND Corporation, 1995.

Moody Jr., Peter R. *Political Change on Taiwan: A Study of Ruling Party Adaptability.* New York: Praeger, 1992.

Morley, James W. *Driven by Growth: Political Change in the Asia-Pacific Region.* Armonk, NY: M.E. Sharpe, 1993.

Morris, Ivan, ed. *Japan 1931-1945: Militarism, Fascism, Japanism?* Boston, MA: D.C. Heath, 1963.

Murray, Williamson and Allan R. Millet, eds. *Calculations: Net Assessment and the Coming of World War II.* New York: Free Press, 1992.

Nahm, Andrew C. *Korea: Tradition & Transformation: A History of the Korean People.* Elizabeth, NJ: Hollym International, 1988.

Naisbitt, John. *Megatrends Asia: Eight Asian Megratrends That Are Reshaping Our World.* New York: Simon & Schuster, 1996.

Neary, Ian, ed. *War, Revolution & Japan Sandgate.* Folkestone, Kent, England: Japan Library, 1993.

Newby, Laura. *Sino-Japanese Relations: China's Perspective.* London: Routledge, 1988.

Norman, E. Herbert. *Origins of the Modern Japanese State: Selected Writings of E.H. Norman.* New York: Pantheon Books, 1975.

North, Douglass C. *Institutions, Institutional Change and Economic Performance.* New York: Cambridge University Press, 1990.

Odom, William E. *Trial After Triumph: East Asia After the Cold War.* Indianapolis, IN: Hudson Institute, 1992.

Odom, William E. *America's Military Revolution.* Washington, DC: American University Press, 1993.

Odom, William E. *On Internal War: American and Soviet Approaches to Third World Clients and Insurgents.* Durham, NC: Duke University Press, 1992.

Oliver, Robert T. *A History of the Korean Peoples in Modern Times: 1800 to the Present*. Newark, DE: University of Delaware Press, 1993.

Olson, Lawrence. *Ambivalent Moderns: Portraits of Japanese Cultural Identity*. Lanham, MD: Rowman & Littlefield Publishers, 1992.

Olson, Mancur. *The Rise and Decline of Nations: Economic Growth, Stagflation, and Social Rigidities*. New Haven, CT: Yale University Press, 1982.

Ozawa Ichiro, Louisa Rubinfien, and Eric Gower. *Blueprint for a New Japan: The Rethinking of a Nation*. Tokyo: Kodansha International, 1994.

Packard, George R. *Protest in Tokyo: The Security Treaty Crisis of 1960*. Princeton, NJ: Princeton University Press, 1966.

Pei, Minxin. *From Reform to Revolution: The Demise of Communism in China and the Soviet Union*. Cambridge, MA: Harvard University Press, 1994.

Pipes, Richard. *Russia Under the Old Regime*. New York: Scribner, 1974.

Pong, David. *Shen Pao-chen and China's Modernization in the Nineteenth Century*. New York: Cambridge University Press, 1994.

Postel-Vinay, Karoline. *Le Japon et la nouvelle Asie*. Paris: Presses de Sciences Po, 1997.

Prybyla, Jan S. "Departures from Communism." *Journal of Democracy*, Vol. 6:3, 1995.

Putnam, Robert D. *Making Democracy Work: Civic Traditions in Modern Italy*. Princeton, NJ: Princeton University Press, 1993.

Pye, Lucian W. *China: An Introduction*, 4th ed. With collaboration of Mary W. Pye. New York: HarperCollins, 1991.

Ramseyer, J. Mark and Frances M. Rosenbluth. *Japan's Political Marketplace*. Cambridge, MA: Harvard University Press, 1993.

Ramseyer, J. Mark and Frances M. Rosenbluth. *The Politics of Oligarchy: Institutional Choice in Imperial Japan*. New York: Cambridge University Press, 1995.

Rees, David. *A Short History of Modern Korea*. Port Erin, Isle of Man: Ham Publishing, 1988.

Renwick, Neil, *Japan's Alliance Politics and Defence Production*. New York: St. Martin's Press, 1995.

Research Institute for Peace and Security, *Asian Security 1995-96*. Tokyo: Research Institute for Peace and Security, 1995.

Rogov, Sergei, "The Reunification of Korea and the Challenges of the Multipolar World," *Korean Unification Significant Issues Series*, Vol. 15:7 (1993): 80-100.

Roy, D., "Assessing the Asia-Pacific 'Power Vacuum.'" *Survival*, Vol. 37:3, 1995.

Royama, Masamichi, *Foreign Policy of Japan: 1914-1939*. Westport, CT: Greenwood Press, 1973 (original 1941).

Samuels, Richard J., *"Rich Nation, Strong Army:" National Security and the Ideology in the Technological Transformation of Japan.* Ithaca, NY: Cornell University Press, 1994.

Savada, Andrea Matles and Willaim Shaw, eds., *South Korea: A Country Study,* 4th ed. Washington, DC: Federal Research Division, Library of Congress, 1992.

Schaller, Michael, *The American Occupation of Japan: The Origins of the Cold War in Asia.* New York: Oxford University Press, 1985.

Schram, Stuart R., *Mao Zedong: A Preliminary Reassessment.* New York: St. Martin's Press, 1983.

Shih, Chih-yu, *The Spirit of Chinese Foreign Policy: A Psychocultural View.* New York: St. Martin's Press, 1990.

Shinn, James, ed., *Weaving the Net: Conditional Engagement with China.* New York: Council on Foreign Relations Press, 1996.

Silberman, Bernard S. and H.D. Harootunian, eds., *Japan in Crisis: Essays on Taisho Democracy.* Princeton, NJ: Princeton University Press, 1974.

Simon, Julian L. and Herman Kahn, eds., *The Resourceful Earth: A Response to Global 2000.* New York: Basil Blackwell, 1984.

Stephan, John J., "Siberian Salient: Russia in Pacific Asia," in *Pacific Century: the Emergence of Modern Pacific Asia.* Edited by Mark Borthwick. Boulder, CO: Westview Press, 1992.

Storry, Richard, *Japan and the Decline of the West in Asia 1894-1943.* New York: St. Martin's Press, 1979.

Storry, Richard, *The Double Patriots: A Study of Japanese Nationalism.* Boston, MA: Houghton Mifflin, 1957.

Stuart, Douglas T. and William T. Tow, *A U.S. Strategy for the Asia-Pacific: Building a Multipolar Balance of Power System in Asia.* Oxford: Oxford University Press for the International Institute for Strategic Studies, 1995.

Stueck, William, *The Korean War: An International History.* Princeton, NJ: Princeton University Press, 1995.

Sun Yat-sen, *Prescriptions for Saving China: Selected Writings of Sun Yat-sen.* Stanford, CA: Hoover Institution Press, 1994.

Sutter, Robert G. and William R. Johnson, eds. *Taiwan in World Affairs.* Boulder, CO: Westview Press, 1994.

Sutter, Robert G. *East Asia and the Pacific: Challenges for U.S. Policy.* Contribution by Larry Niksch. Boulder, CO: Westview Press, 1992.

Swaine, Michael D. and Donald P. Henry. *China: Domestic Change and Foreign Policy.* Santa Monica, CA: RAND Corporation, 1995.

Thompson, Roger C. *The Pacific Basin Since 1945: A History of the Foreign Relations of the Asian, Australasian and American Rim States and the Pacific Islands.* London: Longman, 1994.

Tien, Hung-mao. *The Great Transition: Political and Social Change in the Republic of China.* Stanford, CA: Hoover Institution Press, 1989.

Tilford, Earl H., ed. *Strategic Challenges in an Uncertain World.*

Carlisle Barracks, PA: Strategic Studies Institute, U.S. Army War College, 1996.

Totman, Conrad. *Early Modern Japan*. Berkeley, CA: University of California Press, 1993.

Totman, Conrad. *Tokugawa Ieyasu, Shogun: a Biography*. San Francisco, CA: Heian International, 1983.

Totten, George O., ed. *Democracy in Prewar Japan: Groundwork or Facade?* Boston, MA: Heath, 1965.

Twitchett, Denis and John K. Fairbank, eds. *The Cambridge History of China*, Vol. 14. *The People's Republic, Part I: the Emergence of Revolutionary China, 1949-1965*. Edited by Roderick MacFarquar and John K. Fairbanks. Cambridge, MA: Cambridge University Press, 1991.

Twitchett, Denis and John K. Fairbank, eds. *The Cambridge History of China*, Vol. 15. *The People's Republic, Part II: Revolutions within the Chinese Revolutionary, 1966-1982*. Edited by Roderick MacFarquar and John K. Fairbanks. Cambridge, MA: Cambridge University Press, 1987.

Unger, Danny and Paul Blackburn. *Japan's Emerging Global Role*. Boulder, CO: Lynne Rienner Publishers, 1993.

United States General Accounting Office. *National Security: Impact of China's Military Modernization in the Pacific Region: Report to Congressional Committees*. Washington, DC: General Accounting Office, 1995.

Vogel, Ezra F. *Japan as Number One: Lessons for America*. Cambridge, MA: Harvard University Press, 1979.

Wakabayashi, Bob Tadashi. *Anti-Foreignism and Western Learning in Early-Modern Japan: the New Theses of 1925*. Cambridge, MA: Harvard University Press, 1986.

Walker, Richard Louis. *The Multi-State System of Ancient China*. Hamden, CT: Shoe String Press, 1953.

Weinberg, Gerhard L. *A World at Arms: A Global History of World War II*. New York: Cambridge University Press, 1994.

Wesley-Smith, Peter. *Unequal Treaty 1898-1997: China, Great Britain and Hong Kong's New Territories*. Hong Kong: Oxford University Press, 1980.

Westwood, J.N. *Russia Against Japan, 1904-05: A New Look at the Russo-Japanese War*. Basingstoke, England: MacMillan, 1986.

White, Stephen. *Gorbachev and After*, 3rd ed. New York: Cambridge University Press, 1992.

Whiting, Allen S. *China Eyes Japan*. Berkeley, CA: University of California Press, 1989.

Wilborn, Thomas L. *Japan's Self-Defense Forces: What Dangers to Northeast Asia?* Carlisle Barracks, PA: Strategic Studies Institute, U.S. Army War College, 1994.

Woodrow Wilson International Center for Scholars. *The Cold War in Asia*, Cold War International History Bulletin, iss. 6-7. Washington, DC: Woodrow Wilson International Center for Scholars, 1996.

World Bank. *The East Asian Miracle: Economic Growth and Public Policy*. New York: Oxford University Press for the World Bank, 1993.

World Bank. *World Development Report 1996: From Plan to Market*. New York: Oxford University Press, 1996.

Mary Clabaugh Wright. *The Last Stand of Chinese Confucianism: The T'ung-Chih Restoration, 1862-1874*. Stanford CA: Stanford University Press, 1957.

Wu, Jaushieh Joseph. *Taiwan's Democratization: Forces Behind the New Momentum*. Hong Kong: Oxford University Press, 1995.

Yahuda, Michael. *The International Politics of the Asia-Pacific, 1945-1995*. London: Routledge, 1996.

Yamamura, Kozo, ed. *The Cambridge History of Japan*, vol. 3, *Medieval Japan*. Cambridge, MA: Cambridge University Press, 1990.

Yang, Mayfair Mei-hui. *Gifts, Favors, and Banquets: The Art of Social Relationships in China*. Ithaca, NY: Cornell University Press, 1994.

Yen, Sophia Su-fei. *Taiwan in China's Foreign Relations, 1836-1874*. Hamden, CT: Shoe String Press, 1965.

Yoshino, Kosaku. *Cultural Nationalism in Contemporary Japan: A Sociological Enquiry*. London: Routlege, 1992.

Zhang, Shu Guang. *Mao's Military Romanticism: China and the Korean War, 1950-1953*. Lawrence, KS: University Press of Kansas, 1995.

Zhao, Quansheng. *Japanese Policy Making: the Politics Behind Politics: Informal Mechanisms and the Making of China Policy*. Westport, CT: Praeger, 1993.

ABOUT THE AUTHORS

ROBERT DUJARRIC

Robert Dujarric is a research fellow at Hudson Institute's Washington, D.C., office specializing in international security issues. He joined Hudson in 1993. From 1989 to 1993, he was an associate at Goldman Sachs International Limited in London. Prior to that he was an investment banker with the First Boston Corporation in New York and a consultant to the Investment Banking Department at First Boston (Asia) Limited in Tokyo. He holds a master's degree in public and private management from the School of Management at Yale University and an A.B. from Harvard College. He is the coauthor with William Odom of *Commonwealth or Empire? Russia, Central Asia, and the Transcaucasus,* coauthor with Gary L. Geipel of *Hudson Institute's Executive Briefing,* "Europe 2005: The Turbulence Ahead and What It Means for the United States," and has authored several *Hudson Institute Briefing Papers.*

KIM CHANGSU, PH.D.

Kim Changsu is currently Director, Office of Regional Military Affairs at the Korea Institute for Defense Analyses, a defense think tank affiliated with the ROK Ministry of National Defense in Seoul, Korea. He received his Ph.D. in Political Science from the University of Cincinnati in 1985 and joined the institute that year. Dr. Kim was an APSA Congressional Fellow with the Office of Rep. Solomon P. Ortiz (Democrat for the 27th congressional district of Texas) from 1989 to 1990 and has served as Director, Office of Japan Studies and was also Director, Office of U.S. Studies at KIDA. At present, he is also Editor-in-Chief for the *Korean Journal of Defense Analysis.*

ELIZABETH A. STANLEY

Elizabeth Stanley is a Ph.D. candidate at Harvard University and a MBA candidate at the Sloan School of Management at MIT. She holds a B.A. from Yale University and served for four years as a military intelligence officer in the U.S. Army, including tours in Korea, Germany, and Bosnia. Her publications include *Evolutionary Technology in the Current Revolution in Military Affairs: The Army's Tactical Command and Control System,* (Carlisle Barracks, PA: Strategic Studies Institute, 1998), and a study on the impact of peace operations on force structure and military readiness (Washington, DC: Congressional Budget Office, forthcoming).

LT. GEN. WILLIAM E. ODOM, USA (RET.)

William Odom is a senior fellow and Director of National Security Studies at Hudson Institute's Washington, D.C., office and an adjunct professor at Yale University. From 1985 to 1988, he was Director of the National Security Agency and was responsible for the nation's signals intelligence and communications security. From 1981 to 1985, he served as Assistant Chief of Staff for Intelligence, the Army's senior intelligence officer. He served as Military Assistant to the President's Assistant for National Security Affairs, Zbigniew Brzezinski, from 1977 to 1981. On the National Security Council staff, he worked on strategic planning, Soviet affairs, nuclear weapons policy, telecommunications policy, and Persian Gulf security issues. He graduated from the United States Military Academy in 1954, received an M.A. in political science from Columbia University in 1962, and received a Ph.D. from Columbia University in 1970. He is the author of many books including *America's Military Revolution: Strategy and Structure After the Cold War, Trial After Triumph, On Internal War,* and coauthor with Robert Dujarric of *Commonwealth or Empire? Russia, Central Asia, and the Transcaucasus.*

ABOUT HUDSON INSTITUTE

Hudson Institute is a private, not-for-profit research organization founded in 1961 by the late Herman Kahn. Hudson analyzes and makes recommendations about public policy for business and government executives, as well as for the public at large. The institute does not advocate an express ideology or political position. However, more than thirty years of work on the most important issues of the day has forged a viewpoint that embodies skepticism about the conventional wisdom, optimism about solving problems, a commitment to free institutions and individual responsibility, an appreciation of the crucial role of technology in achieving progress, and an abiding respect for the importance of values, culture, and religion in human affairs.

Since 1984, Hudson has been headquartered in Indianapolis, Indiana. The institute also maintains offices in Washington, D.C., and Montreal, Canada.

Individual and corporate contributors may support Hudson research through tax-deductible gifts to the institute. For information on Hudson programs and publications or for additional copies of this book, please contact Hudson Institute, P.O. Box 26-919, Indianapolis, Indiana, 46226, (317) 545-1000 or fax (317) 545-9639 or www.hudson.org.